The Emergence of Ethical Man

The MeOtzar HoRav series has been made possible by a generous grant from Ruth and Irwin Shapiro.

The publication of The Emergence of Ethical Man *has been made possible by a grant from David Goldberg, as Executor of the Estate of Morton Perl.*

The Emergence of Ethical Man

Rabbi Joseph B. Soloveitchik

Edited by
Michael S. Berger

Published for
THE TORAS HORAV FOUNDATION
by Ktav Publishing House, Inc.

Library of Congress Cataloging-in-Publication Data

Soloveitchik, Joseph Dov.
  The emergence of ethical man / by Joseph B. Soloveitchik ; edited by Michael S. Berger.
    p. cm. -- (Meotzar horav series ; v. 5)
  Includes bibliographical references and index.
  ISBN 0-88125-873-3
  1. Man (Jewish theology) 2. Philosophical anthropology. 3. Bible. O.T. Genesis I-III--
Criticism, interpretation, etc. 4. Charisma (Personality trait)--Religious aspects--Judaism.
I. Berger, Michael S. II. Title.
BM627.S65 2005
296.3'2--dc22
                              2004030917

Manufactured in the United States of America
Distributed by
KTAV Publishing House, Inc.
930 Newark Avenue
Jersey City, NJ 07306
(201) 963-9524
FAX (201) 963-0102
www.ktav.com
Email: bernie@ktav.com

MeOtzar HoRav SERIES:
SELECTED WRITINGS OF RABBI JOSEPH B. SOLOVEITCHIK
Editorial-Publication Board
David Shatz, Series Editor
Joel B. Wolowelsky, Associate Editor
Reuven Ziegler, Director of Research

VOLUME ONE
Family Redeemed
Edited by David Shatz and Joel B. Wolowelsky

VOLUME TWO
Worship of the Heart
Edited by Shalom Carmy

VOLUME THREE
Out of the Whirlwind
Edited by David Shatz, Joel B. Wolowelsky and Reuven Ziegler

VOLUME FOUR
Community, Covenant and Commitment
Edited by Nathaniel Helfgot

VOLUME FIVE
The Emergence of Ethical Man
Edited by Michael S. Berger

Table of Contents

Preface

The Emergence of Ethical Man is the fifth volume of the series *MeOtzar HoRav: Selected Writings of Rabbi Joseph B. Soloveitchik*. Rabbi Soloveitchik *zt"l* (1903–1993) was not only one of the outstanding talmudists of the twentieth century, but also one of its most creative and seminal Jewish thinkers. Drawing from a vast reservoir of Jewish and general knowledge, "the Rav," as he is widely known, brought Jewish thought and law to bear on the interpretation and assessment of the modern experience. On the one hand, he built bridges between Judaism and the modern world; yet at the same time he vigorously upheld the integrity and autonomy of the Jew's faith commitment, and in particular the commitment to a life governed by Halakhah, Jewish law.

For over four decades, Rabbi Soloveitchik commuted weekly from his home in Brookline, Massachusetts to New York City, where he gave the senior *shi'ur* (class in Talmud) at the Rabbi Isaac Elchanan Theological Seminary (RIETS), affiliated with Yeshiva University, and, in his early years there, also taught Jewish Philosophy at the University's Bernard Revel Graduate School. Generations of rabbinical students were taught and inspired by him – among them many of the future leaders of the Orthodox and broader Jewish community. By his extensive personal teaching and influence, as well as by serving locally as the chief rabbinic figure in Boston, where he founded the Maimonides School, he contributed vitally to the dynamic resurgence of Orthodox Judaism in America. The thousands of people who regularly flocked to his public lectures in Boston and New York on halakhic, philosophical and Biblical topics were consistently enthralled and inspired. Rabbi Soloveitchik stands, indeed, as one of the great religious leaders of our time. Even now, after his passing, his teachings – "the Rav's Torah" – are always eagerly sought, and his words continue to ring with relevance and authority.

Although many of Rabbi Soloveitchik's writings and discourses have been published over the years, much additional material, rich and evocative, remains in handwritten manuscripts and recorded tapes. The Toras HoRav Foundation was established by family members and former students to disseminate these and other works, with the aim of enhancing both our grasp of Rabbi Soloveitchik's philosophy and our understanding of the diverse topics he addresses. We congratulate and thank Dr. Michael S. Berger for bringing the Rav's religious anthropology to a long-waiting public.

Alas, it is impossible to appreciate the Rav's powerful and challenging essays without an accompanying sense of the profound loss we have all incurred with the passing of this giant. But the reader who experiences those essays, who absorbs and appreciates their rare blend of intellectual sweep and energizing passion, will find them to be an invaluable, integral part of his or her own spiritual quest.

DAVID SHATZ
JOEL B. WOLOWELSKY

Introduction

'What is Man?' – the central question of anthropology – has pre-occupied thinkers since philosophical reflection began thousands of years ago. From the pre-Socratics and the Hellenistic philosophers through Christian theology and down to Kant, Hegel and the existentialists, explicit answers were sought to the questions of man's place in the world and the nature of his being. And these questions continue to command the attention of Western thought to the present day.

The classic statements of philosophical and theological anthropology still elicit awe and stir the souls of their readers. But it is clear that every normative human system, whether political, social, economic or religious, maintains an underlying view of humanity that animates its worldview. Behind every text that calls man to some action, some belief or some destiny, necessarily lurks a conception of man and how he fits into the complex world around him.

The scientific revolution, ushered in by the Enlightenment, similarly had a conception of man that was a radical departure from the view held by the classical and Christian traditions. Whereas for centuries man had been seen as a unique being, the pinnacle of the created order, according to science he was now merely another element within the vast array of objects and living things that occupy a place in the delicate and complex biosphere we call earth. The theory of evolution epitomized this approach, placing man within the nexus of natural processes – random mutation and natural selection – characteristic of all living things. Humanity thus had no basis to claim axiological pre-eminence over the rest of nature, nor did human beings possess an essential nature that needed to be realized – thus robbing philosophy and theology of the right to make normative claims on individuals. The notion of a goal (*telos*) that humans shared by virtue of their humanity was no longer common coin.

Science, and particularly the theory of evolution, thus put all religious traditions on the defensive. Onto this landscape Rabbi Soloveitchik emerged in the post-war period to carve out the view from Judaism as he understood it. As the Rav wrote in a letter in 1958 to Rabbi Leonard Rosenfeld, head of the Jewish Education Committee of New York, who had been ordained by the Rav's father, Rabbi Moshe Soloveitchik:

> As you know, my interest, at present, lies in the field of religious anthropology, the doctrine of man, within the philosophical perspective of Judaism. It is virgin land. Nothing has been written about the most central problems of human existence, fate and destiny. I am firmly convinced that research in this field would be a rewarding and enriching experience.

Indeed, this subject proved to be an ongoing preoccupation of the Rav. In 1957–58, he offered a series of lectures for the National Institute for Mental Health entitled "The Doctrine of Man," and his "The Lonely Man of Faith" appeared in *Tradition* in 1966. *The Emergence of Ethical Man* (the title was chosen by the editor) is a further effort by the Rav to articulate the concept of man as he saw it embedded in the Bible and the halakhic tradition. For him, Judaism placed human beings firmly within the larger natural order, connecting them to both the plant and animal kingdoms. The critical question for the Rav is how human personality – and the Torah's expectation of moral character and self-transcendence – emerged from such a naturalistic setting. Both the Rav's bold claim and the answer to his question can be found through found through his close reading of Genesis chapters 1–3 and a wide grasp of the Oral Tradition.

In Part I, the Rav sets out to show how Judaism, contrary to both the classical Greek and Christian worldviews, fundamentally sees man as an organic being, subject to the same processes of birth, growth, deterioration and death as other living things, both flora and fauna. In chapter 1, the Rav notes how the account of man's creation is rendered in parallel structure and language to the creation of plants and animals. Indeed, when examined closely, human beings and plants are both highly structured organisms, distinct from their environments, and whose life-systems follow specific rules – all facts Halakhah appreciated and applied in a variety of realms. The unity of men and plants can further be seen in Biblical imagery associating human beings with plants, particularly with respect to growth, reproduction and decay, and in halakhic injunctions against unnatural mixing of species. Finally, Judaism's treatment of the endpoints of life – the embryo and the dying person – shows that man is defined primarily as a dynamic organic being, a full juridical person, regardless of the presence of consciousness.

Moving to the next organic realm, chapter 2 explores the continuity of man with animals, a relation underscored by the Bible's clearly vegetarian tendencies, both in the original creation story, and in the tone of "grudging concession" found in the subsequent license to consume meat in the Torah. It should be underscored that for the Rav, paradise's vegetarianism was a *natural* tendency rather than an *ethical* rule; animals – including man – lacked any drive to consume their fellow creatures. God was the originator and hence owner of all that breathed, so in this regard, human beings and animals were members of the same class. Carnivorousness thus implied "over-reaching," seeking to control and consume that which was beyond human limits and belonged to God. (It is thus no surprise that the consumption of flesh was permitted after the Flood – which punished a generation characterized by violating limits.) In the Torah's ideal world, only God could demand the sacrificial surrender of animal life – all other animal killing constituted murder and the usurpation of divine right. According to the Rav, the sacral system generally, and in particular its insistence on dedicating the first of all growth – plant, animal, and human – are a logical extension of the notion that all life is on a single continuum.

Man's ontic rootedness in his environment makes nature the primary arena for man's moral behavior, says the Rav in chapter 3. Human freedom is embedded in man's coexistence with nature: as long as he lives in harmony with the earth, ennobling his natural existence, then Mother Earth is cooperative; violating natural bounds and frustrating nature's designs, however, leads to alienation from earth – at once defiling the land and forfeiting her blessings. In this very rootedness to place man discovers God; holiness is possible in the location where the divine-human encounter occurs, such as Mount Sinai or the Temple. On the Rav's reading of the Bible, exile from the earth is portrayed as the ultimate punishment for it renders the encounter with God impossible – just as the Jewish return to the land and statehood create the conditions for reconciliation between man and Mother Earth and ultimate redemption. The Jewish view of sin is thus *detachment from* nature, in stark contrast to the Christian notion that sin emerges from man's *attachment to* nature and his natural desires.

Even as man is part of the animal kingdom, in chapter 4 the Rav explores the nature of man's distinctiveness. Even as instinctive behaviors normally satisfy the needs of the *species, individual* animals employ trial-and-error learning and associative memory to achieve their goals. In more complex species of animal life, we begin to notice a directedness in fulfilling these urges, with increasing reliance on technical intelligence to satisfy the animal's needs. This capacity – naturally evolved, not metaphysically bestowed – is most developed in man, and allows Genesis to grant him the supreme position in the created order. But the true turning point in the Creation story is God's address to man to be fruitful and multiply, and to assume stewardship over the earth and creatures. By perceiving himself for the first time as a unique personality, distinct from nature and able to encounter it cognitively as an It, man breaches his immediate and intimate connection with nature that had existed to this point. The divine speech thus brings man to the threshold of personal existence and his emergence as an ethical being – which takes place only in the second account of creation in chapter 2 of Genesis.

In Part II, the Rav studies this emergence of human personality in detail. Chapter 5 begins with the first divine command forbidding Adam to eat of the fruit of the Tree of Knowledge. This decree was pivotal in the story, for it introduced ethical imperatives into the world. Up to that point, man knew only biological motivation; now he had to make a choice in what he ate. Immediately after that, God observes that "it is not good that man should be alone" – a lament that man as an animal lives in solitude, indifferent and neutral with respect to others. By bringing animals before Adam to name them, God seeks to split man-animal and the animal kingdom; the act of cognition – reflecting, classifying and naming the animals – helps Adam confront nature as an object, to sense himself as apart from his environment. But that opposition, in turn, engenders a longing for the solidarity he once shared with the natural world. This is precisely when woman is created: someone who is both different from Adam, but also able to join him in an existential community of two individuals. Procreation is irrelevant here; Eve is the first thou to Adam's I, and in their joint fellowship, man's personalistic nature is fully developed.

Chapter 6 focuses on the emergence of sin as it unfolds in Genesis chapter 3. The serpent's arguments to persuade Eve to eat of the fruit are not simple acts of rebellion; they are radically different portrayals of the experience of God. The serpent sought to depict God not as the purest ethical personality whose will is absolute good, but as a being endowed with highly developed technical intelligence like man, who is therefore locked in competition with man. The prohibition against eating the fruit was motivated by divine jealousy, says the serpent; it was just another attempt by God to enslave man. On this satanic view of God, man – created in the divine image – is bound to become demonic himself. Two personalities – the demonic and the ethical – were now on the Biblical stage, locked in combat.

Indulging in the forbidden fruit of the tree was the first time a human act was motivated not by biological motivation but by the desire for pleasure-experience. The esthetic impulse, where sensual pleasure is paramount, came to the fore when Adam and Eve ate of the fruit, eclipsing the ethical motivations found in chapters 1 and 2. But passion for pleasure is unremitting and ecstatic; satisfaction itself becomes addictive, its grip hypnotic – a point made by Sören Kierkegaard in his own treatment of the ethical and esthetic ways of life in *Either/Or*. The existential union of man and woman (Genesis 1 and 2) that uses sex as a means of achieving this merger of selves gives way in Genesis 3 to a self-obsessed sex-love that turns one's partner into an It, into a source of one's personal pleasure. Sexual life, which could embody ethical solidarity, became an esthetic, hedonic experience of two individuals. By eating of the tree, the first couple took the urge for sex and ethical solidarity and distorted it into a desire for pleasure, for possession and exploitation of one's partner – eliciting unprecedented feelings of sexual shame in man.

The Tree's "Knowledge" was thus hedonic, not cognitive: it awakened lust in man, and was forbidden to him precisely to prevent the pleasure-impulse from dominating human life, to become an end in-and-of-itself. It was this esthetic fascination that led to the subsequent corruption of humanity. By making pleasure his sole objective, man made the entire world his object; and that objectification entailed domination, the insatiable desire to rule over all. Lust, theft, the rejection of authority – all these sins of overreaching stemmed from the demonic personality's hunger for pleasure.

In chapter 7, the Rav deals with the results of the sin in the Garden of Eden. As was noted earlier, the demonic personality sees God in the same terms as man – non-ethical and eager to dominate His creatures. Awe and fear now typify the relationship between God and man; man flees from before this jealous God, and terror necessarily accompanies every instance of divine revelation. The lie, too, is thus invented, for the esthetic personality needed a defense mechanism against the ethical conscience which would not tolerate such self-indulgent behavior. Lying – whether defensively, or even in vain promises – is the echo of the conflict between the torn dimensions of the single human personality: the ethical and the esthetic. Finally, punishment for the sin of pursuing hedonic pleasure is meted out to each sinner: Adam and Eve, severed from their natural environment, will find only pain and suffering in the very esthetic activities they craved, and the serpent is condemned to eternal boredom, absent all joy and pleasure.

Repentance, on this conception, is thus the restoration of the original unity of man, of healing the two parts of human personality – the ethical and the esthetic – that had been severed by the sin in the Garden. This is the basis of Judaism's optimistic view of man, yet the goal requires the charismatic personality, embodied in Abraham and Moses – the subject of Part III.

As the Rav explains in chapter 8, the charismatic personality is always lonely, always a stranger. He must uproot himself from his family, from his society, and from his past in order to develop a bond with God. Abraham was called upon by God to detach himself from the urbanized civilization of Mesopotamia and from its rules to become a nomad, dedicated solely to God. But his anarchism is in service of ethical, not esthetic, ends – a moral law revealed to him by God in spontaneous, prophetic vision and through Abraham's own naturally moral personality. The lonesome God, as it were, enters into a covenant with the lonesome wanderer, and the two become companions and friends. Interestingly, throughout the entire saga of Abraham, God's voice is that of entreaty and request, never command. Abraham offers loyalty and friendship, not surrender. This is the covenant, the bilateral agreement, between God and man. The two thus form an ethical community; God directs and is part of the destiny of His chosen: where they wander, so does He, and where they settle, so does He.

Chapter 9 elaborates on the historical character of charismatic man. God joining the historical drama means that history assumes some of the divine constancy over past, present and future. By covenantally sharing in this historicity, Abraham, the charismatic personality, is able to experience both past events and the mysterious future as the present. He understands that the moral ideal will be realized gradually over time, and therefore organizes a community to connect to the distant past and remote future simultaneously. The original Jewish notion of immortality is not transcendental, but historical: it fuses all dimensions of time. Revelation is experienced by the Jewish community as a current reality, the covenant is reaccepted by each generation, and the historical Jewish people is responsible for the actions of its forebears.

But if the charismatic personality attached himself freely to the promise of the covenant, his descendants who waited for the realization of that promise were forced to live with a historical reality that seriously challenged their faith. The very natural, historical life of the covenant community, the "interim period" between vision and fulfillment, clashes with the teleological aspect of that selfsame community. In the final chapter, the Rav explores Moses' character as a child of this "interim period," who considers God's intentions absurd. But at the burning bush, for the first time the charismatic personality is assigned as a divine agent, for God is duty-bound by the covenant to redeem the people. Man and God must cooperate in the realization of the promise; Moses served both as God's emissary to the people, and as Israel's spokesman before God. This "merger" of the divine and the human in Moses the redeemer begins the reconciliation of the two opposing halves of Adam's personality: the natural and the ethical. Unlike Abraham's harmonious personality, which lacked all tension with the divine, Moses had to re-educate and reform his indifferent personality of the interim period and struggle to turn it into a great harmonious historical personality. As God's agent and executor of the divine will, Moses was able to rehabilitate himself and fuse his dual existence.

As for God, His companionship with Israel and steadfastness through the interim period, followed by His deliverance of the people in fulfillment of the promise, grant Him the title of king and ruler over the Jewish people. Sinai is not a separate covenant, but a new phase in the original covenant with the patriarchs. The people can now become a *"kingdom* of priests" – with God as freely chosen ruler over them – precisely because the divine re-entered history and realized the vision of the original covenant. The Ten Commandments articulate the God-man relationship not in cultic or ritual terms, but in ethical terms that govern social interrelationships, both within society and between man and God. In such a political society, where man and God participate together in the social drama, the gap between them created by the original sin in the Garden of Eden is finally bridged. Once again, man and God are in intimate communion, and man no longer retreats before the terrifying deity.

This book, edited from manuscripts that the Rav kept together but never finished, is further evidence of several lines in his thought that emerged in earlier works. First, the Rav saw in Judaism, and in Halakhah specifically, particular Jewish responses to many universal, existential questions. Halakhah addressed man as a human being first and foremost (a major theme in Maimonidean philosophy); the Rav is thus regularly drawn back to the early chapters of Genesis to mine them for understanding of the condition of universal man, not the parochial Jew. This book should therefore be placed firmly alongside other components of his oeuvre, such as "The Lonely Man of Faith," "Confrontation," and several chapters in *Family Redeemed*, all of which closely read the chapters about creation and find within them profound analyses that speak to all human beings.

Second, the Rav's appreciation for and validation of science as a divine source of truth comes through clearly in this work. Not only was he well-versed in contemporary scientific views, he seems to have been especially interested in how natural science explained the psycho-emotional dimension of human existence. Philosophers and scientists such as Henri Bergson and C.D. Broad, who sought to bridge the growing gap between natural science on the one hand and religion and psychology on the other, drew his attention. The Rav was not prepared to join the chorus of post-Enlightenment religious thinkers who insisted that the spiritual endowment of man was utterly unique, metaphysically unquestionable, and outside the realm of scientific inquiry. Even as he took the divine-human encounter as an a priori assumption, the Rav insisted that every aspect of human personality had to be explained naturalistically, by appeal to the normal interaction of organisms with their environment.

Third, the appreciation for evolutionary processes in both human development and historical progress, particularly in dialectical forms, informs much of this book. Tensions between two antithetical or oppositional forces, particularly in human beings, can be found in virtually every chapter of this work, but the trajectory is clearly towards a synthetic resolution of the conflict rather than merely accepting the tension as irresolvable, an approach the Rav more frequently adopted in several of his later essays.

Finally, a subtheme of differentiating Judaism from Christianity runs throughout this work. Both in Europe and in America, Jewish acculturation extended into philosophical circles, with Jews "translating" their tradition into the Western idiom, which in many cases was shot through with Christian views of the world. The Rav was never comfortable with such "forced conversion" of Jewish thought – a phenomenon which he detected as well in some medieval thinkers, especially Maimonides. In *The Emergence of Ethical Man*, the Rav clearly resists Christianity's lifting of man out of natural history, thus separating the realms of the ethical and the religious from nature. For Judaism, sin results from the esthetic side of man gaining dominance over his ethical side, and redemption results from the successful merger of the historical and the natural.

Taken as a whole, this work is one of the most sustained and thorough readings of the creation story found in Orthodox thought. It is revolutionary in that it breaks with traditional metaphysical categories that are the warp and woof of medieval Jewish commentary and philosophy, and instead bases its analysis purely on the categories of the natural and social sciences. In grounding the halakhic tradition in that alternative nexus, the Rav enables Orthodoxy to take deep and firm root in the intellectual milieu of the modern period – a project he took up throughout his life.

*   *   *

The wealth of unpublished manuscripts Rabbi Soloveitchik left to his family are further testimony to the twin intellectual qualities his students saw on a daily basis for 40 years at Yeshiva University: virtuosity and restlessness. He bestrode the worlds of Torah and Western thought like a colossus, and could draw on both with ease, whether revealing their similarities or highlighting their differences. *The Emergence of Ethical Man* is one of the Rav's most profound contributions in this enterprise, and the assistance of many was required to bring it to publication.

Ten handwritten notebooks, sequentially arranged and bound together yet not ready for publication, formed the material for this book. Rabbi Reuven Ziegler of Yeshivat Har Etzion, director of the MeOtzar HoRav Archives, along with his able staff, skillfully transcribed these manuscripts for editing. The Toras HoRav Foundation honored me with the task of arranging the material into a single work, dividing it into chapters and section headings, choosing chapter titles, locating citations and filling out references, determining what should be text and what should be footnotes, all to assist the reader in the flow of the argument. In many respects, Part II of this work is an elaboration of the opening essay on marriage found in *Family Redeemed*. The Rav's discussion of sexual shame in chapter 6 duplicated several passages in the essays of that first volume of the Rav's works, so we abridged the material here and refer the reader to that work for the full treatment of the subject.

It should be mentioned that the last notebook extended two pages past what is framed as the conclusion of this book. The Rav clearly intended that list of nine points as his summary of the argument to that point before launching into his next subject: man's existential relationship to death, his ultimate fate. However, the writing ends shortly thereafter, and so we decided to let the material up to that point stand on its own as an independent work.

Given the Rav's awesome breadth, the task of editing his manuscripts requires a collective scholarly effort to attain similar reach. First and foremost, Rav Aharon and Tovah Lichtenstein offered both guidance for, and helpful insights to, the entire project. Additionally, I consulted many teachers and colleagues in preparing these manuscripts when encountering difficult passages or references: Drs. David Shatz and Joel Wolowelsky, the editors of the MeOtzar HoRav Series, Rabbis Shalom Carmy, Mark Gottlieb, and Reuven Ziegler, and Professors Elizabeth Bounds, Wayne Proudfoot and David Wisdo.

As the foremost Orthodox thinker of the twentieth century, the Rav saw it as his personal responsibility and lifelong mission to help the halakhically committed Jew live in a Western worldview with intellectual honesty and pride. He resisted facile comparisons and superficial linkages between Jewish thought and the larger world of ideas simply for the sake of integration into the upper echelons of Western culture. For him, living in the modern world afforded Jews an opportunity to express the profound – and highly particular – insights of the Biblical and Rabbinic traditions on all the major issues facing humankind. This work will stand as one of the most significant contributions to that noble enterprise.

Part I
Man as Part of Nature

CHAPTER 1

Man as Organic Being

Two Views of Man

Should we inquire of a modern historian of philosophy or of any educated person well acquainted with the history of ideas what he understands by the word "man," he would immediately advise us about a basic controversy concerning the destiny or essence of this being. By the sheer force of associative thinking, he would at once refer to three disparate anthropological-philosophical viewpoints: the Biblical (referred to by many as the Judeo-Christian view), the classical Greek, and the modern empirico-scientific. Pressed further, he would probably say that the discrepancy between the concepts of man dating back to antiquity – the Biblical and the classical Greek – is by far not as wide as the gap separating those two from the empirico-scientific one. As a matter of fact, he would say, we may speak of some degree of affinity, of commensurability between the Biblical and classical anthropologies. Both are united in opposition to the scientific approach to man: they set man apart from other forms of organic life.

The world of man, these two anthropologies maintain, is incongruous with that of the animal and plant, notwithstanding the fact that all three groups of organic life are governed alike by kindred rigid natural processes and structural developmental patterns. Man is finite and corporeal, yet different; he is not a particular kind of animal. He is rather a singular being. The Biblical and Greek views, of course, disagree as to the distinctive element in man. For the Bible, the mystical image of the transcendental God (*tzelem E-lokim*), as well as the metaphysics of the nous and the logos for Greek antiquity, serve as the ground of man's essential autonomy and his "incommensurability" with other living beings in the ontic realm.

In contradistinction, the modern scientific viewpoint spurns the idea of human autonomy as mythical and unfounded and denies the ontic discrepancy between man and animal-plant. The unity and continuity of organic life is looked upon as an indispensable postulate of all chemical sciences. Man, animal and plant are all placed in the realm of matter, organized in living structures and patterns. The differences between the vegetative-animal and human life concern just the degree of diversity, complexity and organization of life-processes. Life as such is a common grant from nature to all three forms of organic matter, and they share it alike.

As a matter of fact, the contemporary scientific view insists that man emerged very late in the process of organic evolution and thus differs very little from his non-human ancestors as far as his biological existence is concerned.[1] He is an integral part of nature. Even his so-called spiritual activities cannot lay claim to autonomy and singularity. There is no unique grant of spirituality in man. The alleged spirit is nothing but a mere illusion, an appearance, the sum total of transformed natural drives and sense experiences. Spirit, or soul, is reduced to psyche, and the latter – to a function of the biological occurrence.

Indeed, one of the most annoying scientific facts which the

---

1.   The controversy between mechanists and vitalists is impertinent to our problem. Whether life be considered as an accidental end-result of physical and chemical processes similar to those appearing elsewhere, or is a unique endowment of matter whose unfolding is determined by finality, not by accidence, does not alter the implications of the controversy between the scientific and Biblical-classical formulae. Even the staunchest vitalist would accept the scientific thesis concerning the unity and continuity of organic matter. The simplest organism and man are determined by a specific bio-causality.

modern *homo religiosus* encounters and tries vainly to harmonize with his belief is the so-called theory of evolution. In our daily jargon, we call this antinomy "evolution versus creation." The phrase does not exactly reflect the crux of the controversy, for the question does not revolve around divine creation and mechanistic evolution as such. We could find a solution of some kind to this controversy. What in fact is theoretically irreconcilable is the concept of man as the bearer of the divine image with the equaling of man and animal-plant existences. In other words, the ontic autonomy or heteronomy of man is the problem. The Bible and Greek philosophical thought separated man from the flora and the fauna; science brought him back to his organic co-beings.

The ramifications of the controversy between the Biblico-classical and scientific interpretations of man extend into all areas of human philosophic thought. One's theoretical worldview as well as one's practical creed are deeply affected by one's anthropological philosophy. Every axiological system presupposes an understanding of the nature of man, and, of course, the schism between the Biblico-classical and empirical doctrine is of paramount importance to our moral and ethical code. Whether man is a transcendental or a natural being is quite essential to our axiological experience.

However, I wish to emphasize that the widespread opinion that within the perspective of anthropological naturalism there is no place for the religious act, for the relatedness of man to eternity and infinity, is wrong. Perhaps more than man-as-a-divine-person, man-as-an-animal needs religious faith and commitment to a higher authority. God takes man-animal into His confidence, addresses him and reveals to him His moral will. When I said earlier that our axiological experience is interwoven into our doctrinal interpretation of ourselves, I meant to convey the thought that our anthropological view molds our relationship – not to God, but to ourselves. Our self-appraisal and self-evaluation depend upon our self-interpretation. If man is a natural being, the axiological emphasis is placed upon his biological integrity and welfare.

If, however, man is in his essence a spiritual personality, a bearer of a transcendental charisma, be it a universal logos, a free will or a heroic *modus existentiae*, our value judgments revolve about this mysterious ultimate self-reality.[2] Our task now is to investigate the cogency of the almost dogmatic assertion that the Bible proclaimed the separateness of man from nature and his otherness.

It is certain that the fathers of the Church and also the Jewish medieval scholars believed that the Bible preached this doctrine. Medieval and even modern Jewish moralists have almost canonized this viewpoint and attributed to it apodictic validity. Yet the consensus of many, however great and distinguished, does not prove the truth or falseness of a particular belief. I have always felt that due to some erroneous conception, we have actually misunderstood the Judaic anthropology and read into the Biblical texts ideas which stem from an alien source. This feeling becomes more pronounced when we try to read the Bible not as an isolated literary text but as a manifestation of a grand tradition rooted in the very essence of our God-consciousness that transcends the bounds of the standardized and fixed text and fans out into every aspect of our existential experience. The sooner Biblical texts are placed in their proper setting – namely, the Oral Tradition with its almost endless religious awareness – the clearer and more certain I am that Judaism does not accent unreservedly the theory of man's isolationism and separatism within the natural order of things.

The Jewish and Christian Views of Man

Surveying the history of the problem of man's autonomy or heteronomy (which came to the fore long before Darwin, when people were ignorant of evolution),[3] we notice that this problem troubled Christian theologians more than Jewish scholars. The

---

2. Both the classical Greek and the Biblical philosophy of man have branched out into an ascetic practical morality. The Stoa on the one hand and Christian monasticism on the other are characteristic traits of the moral outlook that emerges from the act of spiritualization of man.

3. The psalmist already came across the miracle called man and defined in

naturalistic formula of man was to a certain extent common knowledge among *Hazal,* who did not resent it, while Christian theologians, beginning with Augustine of Hippo and ending with the neo-scholastics, are still struggling with the secularization of human existence by scientific research. The reason lies in the discrepancy between the Jewish Bible and the Christian gospels, the "Old" and "New" Testaments. The Hebrew Bible is cognizant of man as a natural being found on the same plane as the animal and the plant. Indeed, such an idea is a motivating force in Jewish ethics and metaphysics. The nihility, instability, helplessness and vulnerability of man – human life and death – are popular themes of prophets who contrast him with the eternity, unchangeability, everlasting life and omnipotence of the Creator. All those negative traits suggest the naturalness and immanence of man rather than his spirituality and transcendence. Such phrases as

Man is like a breath (Ps. 144:4)

All flesh is grass, and all its grace is as the flower of the field...the grass withers, the flower fades but the word of our God shall stand forever...(Isa. 40:6–7)

so that man has no pre-eminence over a beast: for all is vanity (Eccl. 3:19)

are not epithets of human-divine character. They denote the

---

no uncertain terms his paradoxality and the discrepancy. Sometimes we wonder whether the psalmist did have an insight into man's affinity with nature. "What is man, that You art mindful of him? and the son of man, that You visitest him" (Ps. 8:5). *Ben adam* should be interpreted in the sense of "the son of the earth'" and in the very moment he deprecates man to a low degree in the natural frame of things, he exclaims in rapture, "Yet You have made him a little lower than the angels, and You dost crown him with glory and honor" (Ps. 8:6). Man's autonomy and uniqueness find glorious expression in other psalms: "You turn man back to dust; and say, return, you children of men" (90:3); "You engulf them, they are like sleepers, they

common fate of man, animal and plant, the cycle of birth, growth, deterioration and death. As a matter of fact, the terms *shokhnei batei chomer*, "those who dwell in houses of clay" (Job 4:19), *benei temutah*, "those who are appointed to die" (Ps. 79:11), *ben adam*, *adam*, and *basar* (flesh)[4] all involve the basic concept of man as a natural being. "Death," in Hebrew, *mavet*, applies equally to man and animal – "and if any beast...die" (Lev. 11:39) – and bespeaks the end of the organic process. Man is presented by the prophet under the aspect of temporality which he tries to convert to eternity, of weakness that in his pride man disguised as glory and magnificence. In all this the intimacy and immediacy of man with the physis comes to expression.

The New Testament, drawing on the idea of individual *het* ("sin") which found its full formulation in Ezekiel, shifted man to a different plane and portrayed him in a different light. Man is not any longer the pendulum, that swings between birth and decay, but the being who is torn by satanic revolt, sin and obedience, between living and falling from his God-Father. Both sin and submission are traits related to man as a spiritual-transcendental being. Man-animal can never sin nor humble himself. It is the spirit that revolts, the spirit that submits itself. Man as a biological being is incapable of either. The spirit is in an eternal quest for self-transcendence, to exceed its own relativity and conditionality, and reaches out beyond itself toward regions of absoluteness and indeterminacy.

---

are like the short-lived grass in the morning. In the morning it flourishes, and fades; by evening it is withered and dried" (90:5–6). There is no naturalist who could describe [the] nature of man in more effective and beautiful words. In the metaphor "You engulf them," man is carried by a forceful stream of existence, constituting just a particle of an all-powerful process; the human individual being likened to a flower of the field that blossoms and withers is a most striking presentation.

4. "For all flesh is grass" (Isa. 40:6); "and He remembered that they were but flesh" (Ps. 78:39).

Man's haughtiness becomes for Christianity the metaphysical pride of an allegedly unconditioned existence. Jewish Biblical pride signifies only overemphasis upon man's abilities and power. In view of all that, the New Testament stresses man's alien status in the world of nature and his radical uniqueness. To be sure, all these ideas are not only Christian but Jewish as well. Christianity did not add much to the Biblical-philosophical anthropology. We come across a dual concept of man in the Bible. His element of transcendence was well-known to the Biblical Jew. Yet transcendence was always seen against the background of naturalness. The canvas was man's immanence; transcendence was just projected on it as a display of colors. It was more a modifying than a basic attribute of man.

At any rate, both ideas were considered inseparable by the Bible; Christianity succeeded in isolating them and reducing the element of naturalness to a state of corruption and encountering the transcendent being with an alternative: death or life, while death means transcendental forms of existence and non-existence.

The Christian theologians never tried to reconstruct the story of the creation of man out of the wholeness of creation. Whenever they read the story, they instinctually clung to the verse "Let us make mankind in our image" (Gen. 1:26), and by doing so, they established his supernatural character, his interaction with a transcendental world. They did not dare to tell the story of man in the aboriginal terms of Genesis. Let us analyze this.

The Story in Genesis 1

The story of creation is the biography of nature. The story is not related to any transcendental world or any supernatural phenomena. On the contrary, the Creator is depicted not as transcendent God, who creates a world with which He will never come in contact (what would be a *contradictio in adjecto*), but as *E-lokim*, as the powerful being who dominates all, and who is not at an infinite distance from His creatures. There is no doubt that *E-lokim* bespeaks the dynamics of the world whose source is the Creator.[5] Creation of the earth, light, water, darkness, vegetation, planets, atmosphere (sky), the sun, animals, constitute the main phases of the story. Even the elements with which the Torah begins its story are concrete natural phenomena.

Secondly, the story bespeaks the idea of the unity of the created universe. The emergence of the world by the word of God is presented to us according to a certain principle of order, of a logical dynamic sequence. First Heaven and earth – the frame of the universe – then light, the emergence of the earth-globe, the coming forth of vegetative life, animal, and finally man. The Torah pursues a meaningful pattern of succession; there is no heterogeneity of a disorderly creation. Of utmost importance is the description of the creation of life.

> And God said, "Let the earth bring forth grass, herb yielding seed, and fruit tree yielding fruit after its kind, whose seed is in itself, upon the earth," and it was so. And the earth brought forth grass, herb yielding seed after its kind, and tree yielding fruit, whose seed was in itself, after its kind (Gen. 1:11–12).

> And God said: "Let the waters swarm abundantly with moving creatures that have life, and let birds fly above the earth in the open firmament of heaven." And God created the great crocodiles, and every living creature that moves, which the waters brought forth abundantly, after their kind, and every winged bird after its kind. And God blessed them saying, "Be fruitful and multiply, and fill the waters in the seas, and let birds multiply in the earth" (1:20–22).

> And God said, "Let the earth bring forth living creatures after

---

5. Kabbalists tried to discover allusions in the story of creation to a transcendental order; see Nahmanides's commentary on Genesis 1:1, s.v. *ve-et ha-shamayim*.

their kind, cattle, and creeping things, and beasts of the earth after their kind," and it was so. And God made the beasts of the earth after their kind, and cattle after their kind, and everything that creeps on the earth after its kind (1:24–25).

And God said, "Let us make mankind in our image, after our likeness: and let them have dominion over the fish of the sea, and over the birds of the air, and over the cattle, and over all the earth, and over every creeping thing that creeps on the earth." So God created mankind in His own image, in the image of God He created him; male and female He created them. And God blessed them, and God said to them, "Be fruitful and multiply, replenish the earth" (1:26–28).

And God said, "Behold, I have given you every herb bearing seed which is upon the face of all the earth…to you it shall be for food. And to every beast of the earth, and to every bird of the air, and to everything that creeps on the earth, wherein there is life, I have given every green herb for food" (1:29–30).

These are the generations of the heavens and the earth….And no plant of the field was yet in the earth, and no herb of the field had yet grown: for the Lord God had not caused it to rain upon the earth, and there was not a man to till the ground….And the Lord God formed man of the dust of the ground, and breathed into his nostrils the breath of life; and man became a living soul (2:4–7).

All three reports about creation the of plant, animal and man are almost identical. All three, for example, take account of the common origin of life, namely the earth. All three exponents of living matter emerged out of Mother Earth. Moreover, the fact that man is named Adam bespeaks his origin. The curse of death which was imposed on man after his first sin is founded on the affinity of man with his "Mother" Earth: "...for dust you are, and to dust shall you return" (Gen. 3:19).

It is obvious that man as a divine being, endowed with a transcendental image, is not one with the soil that nourishes him. Adam – man as an earthly creature – is the first man in the Bible. But man is not only identical with the universal source of life, the earth. He is also enmeshed within the entire physical environment. Let us not forget that *ruah* in the Bible means "wind, breath," related to the atmosphere surrounding man. While the Bible's first chapter speaks of *tzelem E-lokim*, "image of God," the second chapter mentions "and breathed into his nostrils the breath (*ruah*) of life" (v. 7). The fact that in regard to vegetative and animal the Bible uses the term *va-yomer* ("said" or "spoke") as the direct command of becoming and in regard to man the *va-yomer* is used in the sense of deliberation should not disturb us much. The same verbs (e.g., *va-ya'as, va-yivra*) are applied to plant and animal in the same manner as in reference to man.[6]

Man in the story of creation does not occupy a unique ontic position. He is, rather, a drop of the cosmos that fits into the schemata of naturalness and concreteness. The Torah presents to us a successive order of life-emergence and divides it into three phases; the last of those living structures is man. The viewpoint is very much akin to modern science. Christianity split the story of creation in two, and analyzed the story of man without taking cognizance of that of animal and plant. That is why it arrived at half-truths and misinterpreted the Biblical anthropology.

The relationships of Jewish scholars and Christian theologians to death will serve as a very conspicuous illustration. Jewish scholars are inclined to accept death as a natural phenomenon that is a part of the biological process (Maimonides, *Guide to the*

---

6. "God *created* (*va-yivra*) the great crocodiles" (1:21); "So God *created* (*va-yivra*) mankind" (1:27); "God *made* (*va-ya'as*) the beasts" (1:25), "Let us *make* (*na'aseh*) man" (1:26). The term *va-ya'as* is used concerning the sky as well (1:7). Of course, *Hazal* noted those peculiarities; see Nahmanides *ad loc.*

Perplexed III:10; Ibn Ezra on Genesis 3:6; Nahmanides, Genesis 2:17 and many statements of *Hazal*), while Christian theologians consider death a punishment for what they term the original sin.[7] We speak of death in a biological sense like the death of an animal, the Bible employing metaphors such as the fading of the flower and the falling of the leaf in the autumn. Christians, in contrast, speak of death as the wages of sin; whoever lives in Christ can never die; Moses died to demonstrate that man is mortal (Romans 6:23, John 11:26).

The conclusion we have reached in our inquiry is both a very simple and very paradoxical one. While the background of man's existence is his involvement in the natural biological occurrence, his vistas are almost endless. His origin is the earth, the mother of the wildflower and the insect; his destiny, destination and goal are placed in the sublime heights of a transcendental world. Man is a simple creature ontically, but a very complicated one ethically. In order to obtain a clear view of the Jewish interpretation of man, we must first find the transition between man's essence and his ideal or, using the jargon of theology, between Adam and *tzelem E-lokim*.

Man as Plant

Let us first analyze the immanence of man, namely his confluence with nature, Mother Earth. As a compass we will use the classical division of reality into four classes: mineral, plant, animal, intelligence (*domem, tzomeah, hai, medabber*), which more or less retains its methodological though not metaphysical significance in modern science. We shall leave out the first phase, that of inorganic matter, which has no relevance for our problem, and start with living matter of the plant. We shall describe tersely two basic

---

7.　The relation of death to sin is a different problem, which needs clarification. Also, the hermeneutic problem of the curse of death which was imposed upon man as penalty for his first act of disobedience engaged the minds of medieval philosophers.

traits of the plant as a representative of life, and compare certain aspects of man with them.

The plant as an organism is a living structure displaying the propensities of change, growth, reclamation, regeneration, and so on. This living structure already displays behavior which bespeaks a within and without, as could only a highly organized system of chemical reactions found elsewhere, or one endowed with a unique functionalism.[8] In the mineral world, it is impossible to speak of an object and its environment or outside; the object is a part of its environment.[9] You cannot say "the table is in contact with its environment"; this would presuppose a within which behaves toward its outside in a certain manner. But we do speak of a structured organism-environment field, and although there is interaction between a living structure and its outside world, we still consider the organism to be a bounded entity, rooted in inner existence. There is reciprocity but also a polarity of within and without.

The second characteristic that I want to distinguish is exactly the polarity of the plant. Functionally it is integrated with its environment.[10] From the purely artistic viewpoint, the flora

---

8. See C.D. Broad, *The Mind and Its Place in Nature* (London: Routledge & Kegan Paul, 1923), who distinguishes between "substantial" and "emergent" vitalism. Gardner Murphy, in his *Personality: A Biosocial Approach to Origins and Structure* (New York: Harper, 1947), discusses Broad's distinction, and states (p. 35):

> Few are inclined today to believe in substantive vitalism, the presence of a life substance or life principle independent of tissue behavior; but there is good reason to believe in emergent vitalism, the genuineness of principles or functions characterizing the life process but existing at no simpler level of organization. In this fashion, the organized living system makes use of one or another physical principle in the world outside, draws upon it and exploits it.

9. The field theory in physics, which dissolved allegedly concrete encapsulated objects into abstract fields of force, accomplished the feat of removing all boundary lines between objects and their environment.

forms a part of the landscape. Whenever we encounter barren arid land, it arouses in us a feeling of discomfort, as if Mother Nature had stripped her clothes. Whenever a painter recreates scenery, it includes the green color of vegetative life. Even from the standpoint of biological functionalism, such an approach is justified. The mere fact that all forms of vegetation are stationary on account of their roots warrants the intimate unity with the environment. The lack of locomotion in the life of plants (except to a very small extent) renders them living structures enmeshed within an outside world. Furthermore, the peculiar capacity of plants for assimilation of inorganic material from the world outside makes them enter into a more outer-inner relationship with their environment. The need for careful selection of food, so pertinent to the animal and man, does not obtain among plants.

Let us now recapitulate the above:

The plant displays two important characteristics that are pertinent to our problem.

(1) *A within-without parallelism.* "The organism exists because outer changes and inner adjustments are nicely attuned" (Murphy, p. 4). In other words, there is an inner-essence existence which behaves toward the outside in a certain fashion. The structured entity must maintain contact with its environment, otherwise it will die. The crystal has absolutely no relationship with the world outside. It is either completely encapsulated or, on the contrary, forms part of the environment. The plant, is on the one hand, bounded as an internal structure; on the other hand, it cannot be isolated

---

10. Of course this confluence of the outside-world and the structure within is not limited to plants alone. It is a universal characteristic of living matter. Biologists speak of an organism-environment field. From a phenomenological viewpoint, the integration of living structure and its environment demonstrates itself more conspicuously on the vegetative plane than on any other plane. Thus, the psalmist speaks of growth as the act of "clothing nature" (Ps. 65:10–14).

from the environment. It has an inner existence, which depends upon an outer world.

(2) Notwithstanding the first characteristic of existence within, the plant functionally and phenomenologically flows together with its environment; the world and the inner structure form one self-nonself.

Let us return to man. The old macrocosm-microcosm idea describing man as a participant in the entire cosmic process may prove useful in regard to our problem. The background of life structure within the structured whole is common to all forms of life, including man. Concerning his entire physiologico-biological functional system – breathing, assimilation of organic matter, circulation of the blood, glandular secretion, and so on – man does not differ from the plant. The same automatic non-teleokeneic (non-self-conscious) functionalism, which operates within man and regulates his response to the outside, prevails in plant. In this regard, man is not to be found one degree above the physiological operation of the plant. We are not cognizant of the functions of our body (what we know we attain by observing others or ourselves as objects) and there is no possibility that man will ever become directly conscious of that physiological performance. There is no act on the part of man concerning those inner-outer functions, which are inherent in the plant.

In contradistinction to the first characteristic which both man and plant share, the second characteristic of the plant's fusion with its environment seems to be unique. Man and animal were granted the capacity for movement, making them more "self-contained" than the plant, which is rooted in Mother Earth. Man and animal must select their food; not everything offered to them by nature is fit for their sustenance. They change places, in search of certain necessities. We cannot speak of them as integrated with a fixed environment. Nevertheless, even they are enmeshed within the outside world and flow into the non-self. Thus, certain viewpoints will tend to bring man closer to his environment on the model of the plant's unity with the outside world; other viewpoints, on the contrary, will strive to grant man more freedom and self-sufficiency.[11]

The Jewish Understanding of Organic Matter

Let us now analyze the Jewish viewpoint regarding the relationship of man-plant by inspecting the halakhic analysis of things organic.

Organic plant life forms one of the most important regions which the Halakhah seeks to understand. In other words, the plant is a halakhic cognitive object. A whole order (*seder*) of the Mishnah deals with *zera'im* (plants). The method which the Halakhah applies in this field is part of the general halakhic methodology:

(1) Halakhic realia; the Halakhah aims at factual descrip-

---

11. Certain philosophies are bent on freeing man from his confinement to a fixed environment. European intellectualism and rationalism and scientific technologism pursue it as a prime objective. Primitive man was more tied in with natural surroundings than the modern *homo sapiens*. Imagining man-brute, we see him enmeshed within a certain environment, be it the jungle, be it the cave. Some philosophies proclaim the ideal of return to nature. Such a controversy finds its echo in political philosophy. The idea of fatherland bespeaks the bond between man and a fixed environment (political and also natural; fatherland is described not only by political attributes but by natural topography). In the last century, European intellectuals thought that one becomes more man in proportion as one dissociates himself from his fatherland. The ideal of cosmopolitanism implies detachment from fixed surroundings. On the contrary, the corporate state-ideal places man within a certain segment of Mother Nature and appraises this as the highest virtue. The method of abstraction, prima facie a logico-epistomological method, is also, at times, a way of living. Man abstracts his own existence from the concreteness of the environment; thus, all those philosophies which saw in intellectual abstractionism the model of cognition display cosmopolitan tendencies. With the return of certain philosophers to the aboriginal sensuous apprehension of reality and with the rehabilitation of the primitive immediacy of naive knowledge, the contact between man and the world outside becomes more intimate. Such a romantic upsurge of man toward primordiality and oneness with the world outside has its effect upon political philosophy (Bergson's *élan vital*, intuition).

tion and causalistic explanation that is based on observation and induction.

(2) Halakhic apriorism. The Halakhah organizes the realia given by observation into halakhic constructs, or a priori schemata, which convert the sensuous data into a halakhic-objective order.

In reference to zera'im, to plants, the Halakhah first interprets the realia in a descriptive and explanatory manner and then tries to fit them into a halakhic matrix.

As to the interpretation of the realia, the Halakhah is extremely objective and scientific. It is concerned with the morphological problem of species and genera. General botanic systematization is a part of the halakhic interpretation. Such a classification is of utmost importance. The concepts of 'kind' and 'species' carry full halakhic validity. The method of systematic description, of abstraction, is similar to that of our general botany and zoology. The Halakhah displays an amazing power of observation of structural details. Morphological patterns and outlines determine the selection of families and groups. The laws of kil'ayim (mixed seeds), of terumot u-ma'asrot (priestly offerings and tithes), of hametz u-matzah (leaven and unleavened bread), hallah (dough offering), hadash (new grain grown before the Omer offering is brought), birkat ha-nehenin (blessings over physical enjoyment), and so on. depend upon the classification of the plant world. The concepts of min be-mino (foods of the same type that mix) and min be-she-eino mino (food of different types that mix together) are basic. Moreover, the Torah characterizes the unique organic existence by morphological group uniformity:

> And the earth brought forth grass, herb yielding seed after its kind, and tree yielding fruit, whose seed was in itself, after its kind (Gen. 1:12).

Organic life begins wherever organized group structural patterns emerge which display propensities of regeneration and growth. But the Halakhah was preoccupied not merely with descriptive morphology but also with explanatory physiology of plants. Growth, food-assimilation, and so on, were central halakhic problems.[12] The term *mei-avira ka-rabi ve-ar'a yanki* (from the air [the plant] breathes, and from the earth it draws sustenance – *Berakhot* 40b) suggests a viewpoint that is quite close to our modern idea. Incidentally, all this was written and formulated in antiquity when the Orient still worshipped the "golden bough" and maintained the myth of the divinity of the tree. Halakhah's approach to the world outside is an objective, mechanistic one: no mythical qualities, no supernatural traits, no animistic dreams. Dead and living matter surrounds us, and this matter must be interpreted in unison with a set of logical principles that will order the given mass of data along lines of continuity and uniformity. Chaos and whim, including transcendental caprice, are inadmissible. The Halakhah looks for stability and lawfulness in this world. Capricious changeability can never be comprehended by the halakhic noesis.

In line with the halakhic interest in the physiology of plants, it occupied itself with the agronomic technique. Methods of cultivation, irrigation, fertilization, symmetry of planting and sowing, constitute the background of *hilkhot zera'im*. The *Mishnayot* of *Orlah* (the first three years of a fruit tree), *Kil'ayim* (mixed seeds), *Shevi'it* (the Sabbatical year) are full of such technical data as *hashka'ah* (irrigation) and *zivul* (fertilization).

The Halakhah studied the plant on three levels: (1) the structural; (2) the physiological; and (3) the technical. On all those levels it observed, described and explained the plant with full understanding for its peculiarity, primordial demands, inner insistences and outer interrelationships. In *zera'im* as in all other

---

12. For instance, the Halakhah sensed the importance of the roots and the leaves for the sustenance of the live plant. Both share the basic function of providing the plant with food. The long-standing halakhic controversy whether a tree's locus follows its roots or its bough (*batar ikkaro azlinan* or *batar nofo azlinan*) is based upon physiological insight. See *Shabbat* 4b and 8a, *Bava Metzi'a* 118b.

regions of halakhic cognitive activity, scientific knowledge of the realia contributes a great deal to the formulation of halakhic formulae and ideas. In some cases it may change our whole halakhic outlook. A trained botanist and agronomist may expose new halakhic aspects in the realms of *zera'im*, *Shabbat*, and so on.

The Uniqueness of the Organic Entity

Not only was the Halakhah acquainted with basic facts of the life of the vegetative world, it also understood the uniqueness of the organic entity. Above, we isolated a paradoxical trait of the plant: it is an internal structure with definite "demands" and patterns which form a bounded unique existence within, responsive to environmental influences that make continuance possible. The organism is closeted structurally and functionally.

Let us see whether the Halakhah accepted such a viewpoint and in what halakhic concepts we find it.

(1) Was the Halakhah cognizant of the plant or even animal as a structured entity that displays singular morphological designs, conceivable only from the aspect of wholeness?

The answer to this question must be given in the affirmative. The idea of an internal structure emerges first in the halakhic term *biryah* (creature, living entity). For instance, wherever the Halakhah requires a specified amount (*shi'ur*), for instance in reference to acts of eating, *biryah* satisfies this demand. Of enormous interest for us is the controversy of Rabbi Shimon and the Sages: while the Sages limited the idea of *biryah* to the zoological realm, Rabbi Shimon extended it to the botanical (*Makkot* 17a). According to both, *biryah* denotes configurative wholeness whose structural organization warrants its existence. It implies the full uniqueness and individuality of each structured entity that renders the additive performance of ours to be absurd. Whereas *shi'ur* means the act of quantitative piecemeal addition to reach a summative result, *biryah* displays qualitative, individualistic traits, morphologically unique outlines that contradict the additive act of assembling parts. No arithmetic operation could combine two individualistic entities into one quantity (*shi'ur*); the term *biryah* denotes aboriginal creature, in contradistinction with artificial synthetic combination. This is synonymous with an organic entity.

In examining the term *terefah* we will derive further conclusions as to the concept of *biryah*. *Basar ba-sadeh terefah lo tokhelu* (Ex. 22:30) translated verbatim would suggest that an animal torn by a beast in the field is unfit for human consumption. Yet the Halakhah identified such a case with the injunction against eating *nevelah*, an animal cadaver that has not undergone halakhic slaughter (*shehitah*). According to the Oral Law, *terefah* denotes something else: a diseased animal. Let us analyze the term *terefah* more deeply. Etymologically, *teref* means "to tear," in particular by a beast: "an evil beast has devoured him; Joseph is without doubt torn in pieces" (Gen. 37:33). However, in Talmudic Hebrew, we already find a metaphoric meaning for *terefah*. Any disturbance or deviation from a planned and charted course, aimless wandering, dominated by accidental forces, derangement of a certain orderly sequence and whenever lawful regularity is superseded by chaos and confusion is described by the word *nitraf*. For example, *nitrefah sefinato ba-yam* means his ship is off her course and her movements are accidental, not directed; *nitrefah da'ato* indicates his mind was deranged; *nitrefah ha-sha'ah* denotes the time became troubled, absurd, confused. Under such an etymological aspect, *Hazal* interpreted the Biblical phrase "*terefah ba-sadeh*" not in the sense of having been torn but rather as being disturbed, abnormal, deformed, incongruous with the morphological patterns of the normal occurrence. In examining the five groups of *terefot*, we find the structural deformity stressed more than the functional disturbance.[13] I would venture to suggest that *Hazal* had an artistic approach to the organic whole. Any distortion of

---

13. Of course, the Halakhah believes that any structural deformity leads to pathological activity of the organic system. Yet the morphological, configurative aspect prevails.

the esthetic, symmetric order was considered an anomaly that belongs to the pathological realm.[14]

This is exactly the point upon which another halakhic concept came to full formulation. The concept of *mum* (defect) denotes exactly a distortion of the organic structural outline whose harmoniously arranged parts must not be disturbed. Any disproportion is classified as a *mum*. Whereas *terefah* signifies a structural-functional anomaly from the viewpoint of organic morphology and dynamics, *mum* refers to any deformity as disturbing the esthetic arrangement of the outline.[15] This is the reason why *mum* is limited to the external organs only, while *terefah* includes both the external and the internal.

(2) Let us now look at the second trait of the plant: its confluence with the environment. Does the Halakhah recognize such integration? We have indicated above that the Bible considers the earth as the spring-well of organic life. The divine act of creation made life spring forth from Mother Earth. Plant, animal and man

---

14. I should stress the difference in the definition of *terefah* in regard to man and animal (cf. Maimonides *Hilkhot Shehitah* 10:12–13 and *Hilkhot Rotzeah* 2:8).

15. Yet, even *terefah* is not completely deprived of the esthetic moment. There need be nothing vague about the matter of esthetic approach to the organism. Organic morphological symmetry is at times synonymous with esthetic harmony. The synthesis of both, organic wholeness and esthetic arrangement, culminates in the concept of *hadar*. The term itself bespeaks an artistic aspect that is inherent in a living structure. If we were to accept Nahmanides' interpretation of *tzelem*, *hadar* in man denotes personal physiognomy. Indeed, we find in Psalms the attribute of *hadar* applied to man: "and You crown him with honor and glory" (Ps. 8:6) and *kavod ve-hadar* bespeaks not concrete symmetry of complex tangible forms but rather an inner quality of beauty expressed in terms of personalism. In reference to *etrog* it points toward structural uniqueness and inner-essence-existence. But in regard to *hadar*, *Hazal* were prompted to use the criteria of *terefah* – "*etrog she-noldu bo simanei terefah*." Such an analogy establishes clearly the parallelism between animal and plant (there are plant structures that can be classified as *terefah*). Secondly, it shows clearly that the Halakhah associates structural organization of the tissues with esthetic unity of form-appearances.

emerged from the mysterious recesses of the earth. This viewpoint prevails in the Halakhah. We identify *gidulei karka* (grown from the earth) with *mehubar* (attached) – whatever is excluded from one category is excluded from the other. The best illustration for such an association is the principle discriminating between plants growing in a perforated pot (*atzitz nakuv*) and those in a sealed pot (*atzitz she-eino nakuv*). With reference to laws relating to *gidulei karka*, plants cultivated artificially are not classified as such: fruit grown in a sealed pot is not subject to all the *mitzvot ha-teluyot ba-aretz* (commandments linked to Eretz Israel); they are *mekabel tum'ah* (i.e., they contract ritual impurity), which any vegetation attached to the ground does not; one who plucks them on *Shabbat* is not violating the Biblical prohibition of reaping and other such acts. The inner motif of such an attitude is that organic life must be confined to a fixed environment, which is identical with the earth. If a plant is placed in an artificially recreated medium, though it meets all the requirements for the sustenance of organic growth, the Halakhah is not inclined to grant it the full status of *gidulei karka*, vegetative living matter. Full-fledged organic activity and creativeness do not yet grant the plant the status of *gidulei karka* so long as it is not rooted in and grown into a fixed environment, Mother Earth.[16]

Etymologically, we find that the word "plant" is closely associated with its locality: *esev ha-sadeh* (grass of the field), *ha-motzi lehem min ha-aretz* (who brings forth bread from the earth), *peri ha-adamah* (fruit of the ground), *peri ha-etz* (fruit of the tree). Thus, vegetative matter always appears in the nominative construct (*semikhut*), inherently attached to the genitive (denoting the environment).

---

16. The controversy concerning a tree which stands within the wall but its branches extend over the wall is characteristic of the halakhic interpretation of the plant-environment field. The Halakhah unifies the loci through the structural unity of *ilan* (tree) and its confluence with the outside world. The reciprocity of plant and locus and their ultimate association eliminates the division of the latter.

Analogy of Man and Plant

Now we shall return to our original problem. Is there an analogue in our philosophical anthropology between man and plant? Does Judaism associate man with the plant?

Let us first analyze the text of the Bible. When the prophets spoke of man, one of their most favored metaphors was the tree. The Torah already associated man with the tree: "for is the tree of the field a man, that it be should besieged by you?" (Deut. 20:19). The translation of the verse is immaterial to our inquiry. Whether we see in this sentence a negative or positive statement, the tree is still the analogue to man. If the verse is affirming this likeness, then it says: "the tree of the field is like the man" – and you are therefore duty-bound to respect its rights and refrain from inflicting any harm. If, on the other hand, we were to read it with the addition of the adverbial "not" ("for the tree of the field is *not* a man"), it almost expresses reverence for a living tree, as if it were a living person. Human beings are at war but not trees; therefore there is no reason why you should besiege the innocent tree and destroy it. It sounds peculiar, almost paradoxical to us, but it was quite natural to the Bible.

Interestingly, the original injunction against wanton destruction (*lo tashhit*) was formulated exclusively in reference to fruit-bearing plants during a siege. The aboriginal motif of this law is that the organic life of the plant is not subject to destruction, even as human life is being annihilated. We have the impression as if the Torah placed the "murder" of trees above the slaughter of humans! Something else is worth noticing. I am not supposed to destroy plants even if this act of destruction would accelerate the fall of the city. The tenderness and love with which the Torah surrounds the helpless tree is paradoxical, though very revealing as to our attitude toward organic still life.[17]

Man-plant metaphors fill the prophets' speech. Sometimes

---

17. See Leopold Löw, *Gesammelte Schriften*, ed. Immanuel Löw (Szegedin: Alexander Bába, 1889), vol. I, p. 67 ("Der Baum").

man is compared to a tree planted by the rivers of water,[18] to a green olive tree, to the cedars of Lebanon, to the flourishing grass, to the fruitful vine, and so on. The likeness of man to plant is the most central theme in the prophets. And this runs both ways, the negative and the positive. Man's short-lived sojourn on earth, his weakness, vulnerability and exposure to the elemental forces of nature are pictorially described by using the analogue of the plant, which displays similar qualities. On the other hand, the propensities of the plant to grow rapidly and in multitudes, to regenerate, to repair its losses, were used by the prophets in their vision of the glorious future of Israel and of the righteous individual. The drama of the rebirth of life that recurs every spring suggested to the prophet the great hope of rejuvenation of his people Israel. The motivating idea is the mysterious intimacy and immediacy of man with the flourishing and fading plant.

But is it only a metaphor, a beautiful phrase? Does it contain an eidetic, an unusually vivid, photographically exact kernel, that is unique in the Jewish anthropological formula? Let us turn to the Halakhah!

As we stressed above, the attribute of group-belonging that is the basis of any general classification was given by the Torah to vegetative life:

> And God said, "Let the earth bring forth grass, herb yielding seed, and fruit tree yielding fruit after its kind, whose seed is in itself, upon the earth," and it was so. And the earth brought forth grass, herb yielding seed after its kind, and tree yielding fruit, whose seed was in itself, after its kind…(Gen. 1:11–12).

The plant is described by the Torah as having three unique qualities: (1) growth (*tadshe*); (2) reproduction (*esev mazri'a zera*);

---

18. "And he shall be like a tree planted by streams of water, that brings forth its fruit in its season" (Ps. 1:3).

(3) group identity that is carried through the mechanism of heredity (*oseh peri le-mino*). The propensity of regeneration and group identity emerge later as characteristics of animal life.

> And God created the great crocodiles, and every living creature that moves, which the waters brought forth abundantly, after their kind, and every winged bird after its kind. And God blessed them saying, "Be fruitful and multiply, and fill the waters in the seas, and let birds multiply in the earth" (Gen. 1:21–22).

> And God made the beasts of the earth after their kind, and cattle after their kind, and everything that creeps on the earth after its kind; and God saw that it was good (1:25).

Concerning man, the Torah did not mention group affiliation for a simple reason: it believed in the equality of all men. The differentiation of men into groups occurs later, after the incident of the Tower of Babel, prompted by social and economic forces. However, the second characteristic of plant-life, namely, reproduction, applies to man as well: God said to them, "Be fruitful and multiply, replenish the earth" (1:28). Of course the Halakhah converted this trait into a norm. Yet this interpretation does not change the basic fact that multiplication as such is derived from the vegetative mode of organic life. It is not an exclusive privilege of man.

Yet even in regard to the group-differentiation, we may find some application of that trait to man. Nahmanides (Lev. 19:19) already pointed to the affinity of the prohibition against mixing species (*kil'ayim*) to the quality of group-belonging with which God endowed plants and animals at the birth of organic life. There is no doubt that he has hit upon the raison d'être of the prohibition: the Torah looks askance at artificial changing of the group-traits and group demands and insistences. Again, we find *kil'ayim* applicable to plant and animal alike. Unnatural mating for the purpose of developing an organic hybrid culture was prohibited. The Torah sees in such an act an attempt on man's part to interfere with the structural and functional patterns that are inherent in organic systems and to bring about unnecessary mutations of forms. The Torah calls such an act *hashhatah* (corruption, deterioration, destruction): "for all flesh had corrupted its way upon the earth" (Gen. 6:12).

A similar injunction we find in regard to man, though halakhically it is not formulated as *kil'ayim*: bestiality and homosexuality. Both are considered unnatural acts. The first one enjoins man from carnal copulation with a mate that does not belong to his kind. The second one prohibits any sexual relationship between male and male, for by the laws of nature, established and sanctioned by the act of creation, mating is a male-female relationship.

Again both motives are not to be found exclusively in the realm of man, but in organic life as such. Man should behave like the plant in its natural environment, whose fruition is automatic (by the wind or insects) and follows a certain uniform, pre-established sequence. It is worth mentioning that both prohibitions (bestiality and homosexuality) apply to non-Jews too and form part of a universal religion that is based upon the concept of man and personality.

Man as Organic Being

Let us now state further that the Halakhah, in formulating the idea of man, was many a time guided by the idea of man as an *organism* that displays a certain drive, though elemental and unconscious, toward existence in communion with the outside.

It comes to the fore in halakhic formulas and principles. Had the Halakhah accepted another anthropological criterion, it would have operated either with the Greek logos consciousness or with the so-called Biblical *tzelem*. Yet the Halakhah identifies man with the biological form of existence – the dynamic organism.

Let us first consider the laws pertaining to the endpoints of life: the embryo and the *goses* (individual on the brink of death).

Turning to the beginning of life, even the embryo in the womb is considered under many aspects a person endowed with juridic prerogatives. The murder of an unborn child is classified as a crime, which is punishable with *mitah biydei shamayim* (death at the hands of Heaven); indeed, even a non-Jew is executed for killing fetuses.[19] Whenever the life of the unborn child is endangered, the law of *pikuah nefesh* (saving life) is applicable according to the opinion of many *Rishonim* (Nahmanides disagrees). Even in case of an abnormal birth, when the physician is allowed to sacrifice the unborn baby for the well-being of the mother, Maimonides introduces the motif of *rodef* (pursuer). The physician is instructed to save the mother because the child is classified as a *rodef*. Otherwise it would be prohibited to prefer the life of the mother to his.

Now let us turn to the *goses*. A man in the state of coma possesses all the rights with which the human being is endowed. Whoever inflicts harm is liable for the act. The slaying of a *goses* is synonymous with the murder of a healthy sane person. Moreover, he may acquire property (he is not only a physico-chemical reality but also a juridic one), he still exercises control over his pos-

---

19. *Sanhedrin* 57b; Maimonides, *Hilkhot Melakhim* 9:4. According to Christianity and its mythical theory of a twofold birth, man actually attains his status at the baptismal ceremony. Man is a metaphysical being and this distinction is granted to him through a ceremonial act replete with mystical significance. The natural birth does not endow him with that uniqueness and sanctity. Some other performance is necessary for his elevation to the spiritual heights of a divine being. Such a philosophico-anthropological formula has influenced the history of the Church throughout the ages. The bloody chapter of the Inquisition was an outgrowth of such a misinterpretation of man. If the natural being is not worthy of his Creator and only his metaphysical transfiguration makes him what he is, then a man outside of Mother Church may not lay claim to the rights and prerogatives of the metaphysical man. The metaphysical rebirth is a prerequisite for granting man the privileges implied in the idea of *tzelem*. Even murder may be committed on a heretic for he does not share the spirituality, the uniqueness of man, "for in the image of God, made He man" (Gen. 9:6). Immortality is again limited to the metaphysical being. The natural is excluded.

sessions and no one can deprive him of this privilege. Halakhah does not recognize incompetence as a cause for cancellation of juridic prerogatives.

Furthermore, we have a controversy in Halakhah whether *ha-mezakeh le-ubar kanah*, i.e., whether an unborn child has civil rights, like the right of acquisition or that of inheritance. In regard to the laws mentioned earlier, we could say that though the Halakhah does not define personality in naturalistic, biological terms, it still considers an embryo and a *goses* potential and past personalities, respectively. However, we cannot interpret civil rights under such an aspect. An embryo as a "juridic person" bespeaks an actual person, not a prospective one. There is not a single opinion in the Talmud that tends to deprive the *goses* of his civil rights and juridic qualifications. If the Halakhah had identified the idea of man with that of consciousness, logos, intellectual activity, as Maimonides did under the impact of the Greek philosophical anthropology, then neither the embryo, nor the newborn, nor the man in the comatose state could be considered under the aspect of juridic person. Let us not forget that the embryo or the dying man deprived of all faculties resembles the plant far more than the animal. Instinct, sensation, active response to stimuli, locomotion, and many other neurological processes that characterize animal existence are completely extinct in such persons. And still, man remains man. Halakhah considers this purely vegetated form of life, projected upon an anthropic background, as a manifestation of a personality. It sounds bizarre, yet the Halakhah saw in the budding of organic life the outline of a personality, endowed with many personalistic attributes.

Yet the problem of man-plant has not yet been solved.

CHAPTER 2

Man as a Carnivorous Being

The Vegetarian Nature of Creation

Let us analyze the halakhic attitude toward man's communion with the organic world. For the sake of expediency we will examine the relationship that the Halakhah intended to establish between him and the animal. There is a distinct reluctance, almost an unwillingness, on the part of Torah to grant man the privilege to consume meat. Man as an animal-eater is looked at askance by the Torah. There are definitive vegetarian tendencies in the Bible. This sounds, prima facie, a little absurd. Yet if we disregard conventional opinions and attempt to penetrate into the substrata of halakhic philosophy we detect such ideas.

As the story of creation relates, only vegetarian food was assigned to primordial man. The Bible discriminates very little between man and animal in reference to food:

> And God said, "Behold, I have given you every herb bearing seed which is upon the face of all the earth... to you it shall be for food. And to every beast of the earth, and to every bird of the air, and to everything that creeps on the earth, wherein there is life, I have given every green herb for food": and it was so (Gen. 1:29–30).

Man, like animal, was created originally to live solely upon vegetables and fruits. Let us be clear that this rule was not given to man as an ethical norm but as a natural tendency; it is absurd to speak of a law imposed upon "every beast of the earth, and to every bird of the air, and to everything that creeps on the earth." Since they are mentioned together with man, we may safely conclude that this injunction was a physiological pattern that dominated man's sensory drive, not an ethical imperative. Primordial man neither desired nor was tempted by any food other than of the vegetative realm. Thus, the verse concludes "and it was so": the ethical norm became a behavior pattern, an expression of the ontic order. Man and animal were not driven toward killing or devouring other living creatures.

Somehow – the reason is irrelevant to our present inquiry – nature deteriorated. The Torah states unequivocally that all flesh became wicked:

> And God saw that the wickedness of man was great in the earth, and that every imagination of the thoughts of his heart was only evil continually (Gen. 6:5).

> And God looked upon the earth, and behold, it was corrupt; for all flesh had corrupted its way upon the earth (6:12).

This condemnation extends to all living things. Therefore, God decrees death upon all creatures: man, beast, creeping worm and fowl of the air. All were base and corrupt.

> And the Lord said, "I will destroy man whom I have created from the face of the earth: both man, and beast, and creeping things, and the birds of the air, for I repent that I have made them" (6:7).

All flesh had corrupted its way upon the earth, so all deserved to be ruthlessly exterminated.

What was the nature of this "corruption"? Apparently, the word *hishhit* implies not only ethical corruption, but natural as well. All creatures had overreached themselves. Certain processes developed that changed the nature of animal and man. These creatures acquired new drives and began to display new demands that exceeded the limits set by divine will and aboriginal, undisturbed nature. They began to stretch their hand out to something that did not belong to them, to alien property. They began to rob, to grab, to reach for somebody else's goods, to strip others of their rightful possessions. This going after something which is beyond one's jurisdiction and ontic sphere is called *hamas*.[1] *Hamas* is the universal act of interfering with somebody else's right and prerogatives, usurping something that is not mine, the act of overreaching oneself and reaching out to the non-self. *Gezelah* (theft) is a specific case of *hamas*, in which concrete goods are taken away from their rightful owner.

> ...that the *benei ha-elohim* ("distinguished men") saw that the daughters of men were fair; and they took them for wives of all whom they chose (Gen. 6:2).

Apparently, one of the *hamas* acts was the reaching out of man and animal after the lives of other creatures inferior to them in physical strength. For the first time there emerges the division of the species into *teme'ot* (impure animals) and *tehorot* (ritually pure animals), an allusion to a basic change in man's relationship to animal. Paradoxically he overreached himself, created a new demand, a sinful insistence upon something which by right does not belong to him, namely, on life that is equal to his, on flesh that is not different from his own, and he succeeded. God, as it were, gave in and compromised with man:

---

1.   See *Sefer ha-Shorashim* of R. David Kimhi, s.v. *h.m.s. Hamas* denotes deviation from the right path, removing objects from their place, corruption, an anomalous performance, destruction.

> And God blessed Noah and his sons and said to them, "Be
> fruitful, and multiply, and replenish the earth. And the fear
> of you and the dread of you shall be upon every beast of the
> earth, and upon every bird of the air, upon all that moves
> upon the earth, and upon all the fishes of the sea; into your
> hand are they delivered. Every moving thing that lives shall
> be food for you; even as the green herb have I given you all
> things" (Gen. 9:1–3).

A new relationship is established between man and animal, tension engendered by fear and dread. Animal is afraid of man, flees before him. Why? Because he has lost confidence in man; instinctively, he feels animosity, evil designs, on the part of man. Here the revolutionary change is clearly formulated. "Into your hand are they delivered. Every moving thing that lives shall be food for you." Man-animal became a life-killer, an animal-eater. He became bloodthirsty and flesh-hungry.

Is the Torah very happy about this change? Somehow we intuitively feel the silent tragic note that pervades the whole chapter. The Torah was compelled to concede defeat to human nature that was corrupted by man himself and willy-nilly approved the radical change in him. *Hamas*, reaching out after a life, became habitual with man. At once the Torah began to regulate the "murder" of other lives, to restrict its practice by complicating its procedure. *Hazal* formulated this tendency in their famous maxim:

> The Torah only provided for human passions: it is better for
> Israel to eat the flesh of animals that are ritually slaughtered
> than the flesh of animals which have perished (*Kiddushin*
> 21b–22a).

A concession was made to an evil drive brought about by ontic deterioration. All the laws of prohibited foods must be seen under this aspect. The continuation of that chapter is remarkable:

> But flesh with its life, which is its blood, you shall not eat. And
> surely your blood of your lives shall I require.... Whosoever
> sheds man's blood by man shall his blood be shed (Gen.
> 9:4–6).

"Though I have permitted the killing of the animal, you shall not
consume the flesh with the soul – that is, the blood – thereof."
The first ban was placed by God on consumption of meat cut off
a live animal, "*ever min ha-hai.*" The Torah continues "And surely
your blood of your *lives.*" Though I reluctantly approved of taking
animal life in order to satisfy your carnal desire, I prohibit murder
of your own kind.

Of special interest is the fact that the injunction against meat-
consumption was canceled after Noah brought his first sacrifice.

> And Noah built an altar to the Lord; and took of every clean
> beast and of every clean bird, and offered burnt offerings on
> the altar. And the Lord smelled the sweet savor; and the Lord
> said in His heart, "I will not again curse the ground any more
> for man's sake; for the impulse of man's heart is evil from his
> youth; neither will I smite anymore everything living; as I
> have done" (Gen. 8:20–21).

> And God blessed Noah... and the fear of you and the dread
> of you shall be upon every beast (9:1–2).

The new privilege granted man is a consequence of his evil intentions and is closely associated with the sacrificial act. The last
point needs elucidation.

The Torah's Attitude Toward Meat-eating

Let us examine the attitude of the Torah toward flesh-eating as
displayed in the Sinaitic laws. The story in Numbers about the
complaints of the Israelites concerning the manna, their demand

for a variety of food and the divine response to their murmurs and grumbling gives clear evidence of the dislike the Torah displays for those meat-eaters.

> And the mixed multitude that was among them fell a lusting: and the children of Israel also wept again, and said, "Who shall give us meat to eat?" (Num. 11:4).

The Torah has one name for such a desire: *ta'avah*, lust, illicit demand.

> And say to the people, "Sanctify yourselves against tomorrow, and you shall eat meat: for you have wept in the ears of the Lord saying, 'Who shall give us meat to eat? for it was well with us in Egypt.' Therefore the Lord will give you meat and you shall eat. Not one day shall you eat, nor two days, nor five days, nor ten days, nor twenty days, but a whole month, until it come out at your nostrils, and it be loathsome to you: because you have despised the Lord" (Num. 11:18–20).

So much disdain and contempt we find in no other story. The insistence upon flesh, this lusty carnal desire, arouses divine wrath.

The tragic sequel to this story is very characteristic:

> And while the meat was yet between their teeth, before it was chewed, the wrath of the Lord was inflamed against the people, and the Lord smote the people with a very great plague. And He called the name of that place *Kivrot ha-Ta'avah* (Tombs of Lust), because there they buried *the people that lusted* (11:33–34).

Animal hunters and flesh-eaters are people that lust. Of course it is legalized, approved. Yet it is classified as *ta'avah*, lust, repulsive and brutish.

The real motif that prompts such an unquestionable antagonism toward slaying of animals is the aboriginal Jewish thought that conceives man on a natural-vegetant-animal plane. Particularly man and animal are almost identical in their organic dynamics that is equated with life, and there is no justifiable reason why one life should fall prey to another. Why should a cunning intelligence that granted man dominion over his fellow animals also give him a license to kill?

Yet we must continue with our inquiry into the Torah's attitude toward flesh-eating.

Sacrifices

The first half of Leviticus is devoted to *korbanot* (ritual sacrifices), dealing with them in great detail. Slaying animals in a non-sacred manner is not even mentioned. All we read is about offerings.

In chapter 17, we find a strange discussion. Following Nahmanides, the first seven verses refer to *besar ta'avah*, meat eaten out of carnal desire, while verses 8 through 12 deal with *shehutei hutz*, the slaughtering of a consecrated animal outside the Tabernacle's precincts. According to the view of Rabbi Ishmael, non-consecrated meat was forbidden in the wilderness:

> Any man of the house of Israel who kills an ox, or lamb, or goat, in the camp, or who kills it outside the camp, and brings it not to the door of the Tent of Meeting, to offer an offering to the Lord before the Tabernacle of the Lord; blood shall be imputed to that man, he has shed blood, and that man shall be cut off from among his people (Lev. 17:3–4).

Non-ceremonial taking of animal life was forbidden. Only sacral killing of an animal was sanctioned:

> To the end that the children of Israel may bring their sacrifices, which they offer in the open field, that they may bring them to the Lord, to the door of the Tent of Meeting, to the priest, and offer them for peace offerings to the Lord (17:5–6).

The animal is designated by divine law as an offering to God.[2]

In Deuteronomy the Torah made an exception to the rule and permitted *besar ta'avah*. The reason for the liberalization of the ritual was the change of conditions.

> When the Lord your God shall enlarge you border, as He
> promised you, and...you long to eat meat; you may eat meat,
> to your heart's desire (*te'aveh nafshekha*). If the place which
> the Lord your God has chosen to put His name there be too
> far from you, then you shall kill of your herd and of your
> flock...and you shall eat in your gates to your heart's desire
> (*avat nafshekha*) (Deut. 12:20–21).

The Torah explains the reason for the modification of the old prohibition: with the centralization of the Temple worship in Jerusalem, limiting slaughter to ceremonial acts would prove an impossible hardship. Nevertheless, the Torah again calls a desire for meat *ta'avah*, lust; while the Torah tolerates it, it is far from fully approving it.[3]

Finally, at the conclusion of both passages in Leviticus and Deuteronomy, the Torah sternly prohibits the consumption of blood; and in both, the Torah is ruthless in its condemnation of the blood-eater:

> And whatever man there be of the house of Israel, or of the
> strangers that sojourn among you, that eats any manner of
> blood: then I will set my face against that person that eats
> blood, and will cut him off from among his people. For the

---

2. Only those species that are not fit for sacral rites can be killed: "And whatever man there be of the children of Israel, or of the strangers that sojourn among you, who hunts venison of any beasts or bird that may be eaten, he shall even pour out its blood, and cover it with dust" (Lev. 17:13).
3. See Rashi *ad loc.*: "But in the wilderness, meat was prohibited to them unless it was sanctified and offered as a peace-offering."

life of the flesh is in the blood: and I have given it to you upon the altar to make atonement for your souls: for it is the blood that makes an atonement for the soul (Lev. 17:10–11).

Only be sure that you eat not the blood: for the blood is the life; and you may not eat the life with the meat. You shall not eat it, you shall pour it on the earth like water. You shall not eat it, that it may go well with you, and with your children after you, when you shall do that which is right in the sight of the Lord. (Deut. 12:23–25).

The phrase "then I will set my face against that person" – meaning I shall single him out – occurs only twice in the Torah: here and in forbidding child-sacrifices.

And I will set my face against that man, and will cut him off from among his people; because he has given of his seed to Molech, to defile my sanctuary, and to profane my holy name (Lev. 20:3).

Obviously, the Torah looks upon blood-eating with so much horror and abomination that it is almost placed on a par with the worship of Molech. What is the reason for such an attitude? The Torah itself explains the reason.

For the life of the flesh is in the blood: and I have given it to you upon the altar to make atonement for your souls: for it is the blood that makes an atonement for the soul. Therefore I said to the children of Israel: none of you shall eat blood (Lev. 17:11–12).

Because blood is the very essence of life and as such it must be consecrated as a sacrificial offering to God, "that is why I enjoined the Israelites from eating blood."

The Torah's expression in Leviticus is unique, and truly remarkable:

> Whosoever...kills an ox, or lamb, or goat...and brings it not
> to the door of the Tent of Meeting to offer an offering...blood
> shall be imputed to that man, he has shed blood, and that
> man shall be cut off from among his people (Lev. 17:3–4).

The implication is clear: whoever kills an animal for non-sacramental purposes is guilty of bloodshed, of murder; the term *shefikhut damim* applies equally to the slaughter of man and animal. Under a certain aspect, the life of the animal has been placed on an equal plane with that of man. Why?

God as Owner of All Life

When the Bible contrasts the God of Israel with the gods of the pagan world, the prophets make use of two divine attributes: the God of Israel is the *maker* and *creator* of the universe, while the other gods are man-made; hence the God of Israel is a *living* God, while the pagan gods are non-living, dead, hewn out of stone or carved out of wood.

> ...eyes have they, but they cannot see; ears have they, but
> they cannot hear; noses have they, but they cannot smell
> (Ps. 115:5–6).

Seen a bit deeper, both attributes are synonymous for the prophets. Omnipotence signifies life, incapacity and inability bespeak lifelessness, death. Furthermore, omnipotence denotes not only the ability to *perform* within the cosmic and social drama, but also the ability to *respond*, to react to certain events taking place in this world and to act accordingly. In other words, life implies not only free creative initiative prompted by unique, autonomous motives, but responsive inner drive, determined and conditioned by the world without. (We stressed this peculiarity in describing life in its primordial manifestation in the realm of plant.) The living being in his relationship to his environment is both affecting and being affected. This bi-directional interaction is the foundation of living.

Hence, since God is living, this double criterion had to be applied to Him. God is not only the absolute, autonomous creator of the cosmos, but also the onlooker, before whom the whole cosmic drama unfolds and who responds and reacts to change. He sees the world in its multi-colored, eternal beauty and in its repulsive abomination and ugliness. He listens not only to the music of the spheres and the hymn-singing of heaven and earth – "the heavens declare the glory of God; and the firmament proclaims His handiwork" (Ps. 19:2) – but to the wailing of the oppressed and persecuted, to the hollow and pained voices of injustice and violence. God loves and hates; God is saddened and gladdened; God likes and dislikes. God is not only the active creator but also the passive sufferer of the cosmic drama. The Bible is very far from sharing the views which were later espoused by the medieval philosophers in their tireless crusade against any anthropomorphism. By assigning to God pure actuality to the exclusion of all responsive behavior, one detaches Him from His world and renders practical religion almost absurd.

We have seen that life in the natural-organic realm is not something in *toto genere* different from divine life. On the contrary, all life is rooted in God and can be traced to Him. "Life" in the Bible is a unique attribute of God that conveys the real essence of Him. If there is life in a creature, it is because God grants a spark of His own living being to the world.

> …and [God] breathed into his nostrils the breath of life; and
> man became a living soul (Gen. 2:7).

In a rather naturalistic description, the man became a living soul because God blew in his nostrils the breath of life – nothing is told here of *tzelem*. Man breathes with God's *nishmat hayyim* (breath of life); man lives by it and through it.[4]

Hence, a new concept evolves. *All* life is considered by Judaism as belonging to God. He has exclusive, absolute ownership rights to all living creatures, to everything that has been redeemed from lifelessness and dead matter, and raised to the plane of life. God holds every living being in His private ownership and exercises full dominion over it. Even as the whole universe is held by God, there is a unique juridic relationship of possession and dominion to life. All living beings enjoy only the rights of tenancy; they do not exercise dominion over their holdings. This tenancy may become extinguished at any time; the freeholder may be dispossessed of his temporary rights. There is no contractual legal protection of the tenant against the will of the owner. The latter has the sole right of possession and dominion, and while He granted His creature some lease on life, He did not relinquish juridical power and control over it. On the contrary, the living being owes Him unequivocal allegiance; any sin or error renders the whole relationship void. Man and animal forfeit their relative, conditioned rights by the slightest error or offense. Any failure to perform their servitudinal obligation exposes them to the danger of losing their existence. Life of finite, temporal beings is rooted in the life of the infinite, eternal being. The ebbing of life is synonymous with the waning of the divine breath. The union begins to dissolve.

> For She'ol cannot praise You, death cannot celebrate You;
> they that go down into the pit cannot hope for Your truth
> (Isa. 38:18).

---

4. Prophecy – closeness of man to God – is described as *ruah Hashem* ("God's wind" or "God's breath"). When man's breath, the criterion of life, becomes one with the divine breath, prophecy comes into action.

I will walk before the Lord in the land of the living
(Ps. 116:9).

The concept of *korban* (animal sacrifice) flows directly from these metaphysico-mystical springs. Every life is indebted to God, is held by God absolutely and must surrender itself upon demand. And indeed, God demands sacrifices, including the very life of man. The pagan ritual of human sacrifice was prompted by a motif which was basically true. The error of paganism consisted in separating the ethos from the cult. Ritual demands human sacrifice; the ethos, appreciating life as precious, forbids. Judaism was the first religion that combined both and therefore introduced basic changes in the idea of *korban,* sacrifice, stripping it of its barbarism. We evolved the substitution for the human sacrifice by the physical sacrifice in general, by mental and spiritual surrender to God.

However, no one is allowed to destroy organic life. Murder is usurpation of something not belonging to me, the act of interfering with exclusively divine prerogatives.[5] Murder is *hamas,*[6] for I rob another person of his life which was granted to him by God.

Whosoever sheds man's blood, by man shall his blood be
shed: for in the image of God made He man (Gen. 9:6).

Tzelem actually signifies life as a divine grant to man. By slaying man, the murderer is committing *hamas,* taking illegitimate possession of divine rights.

Only God, who gives life, can take life away. "The Lord kills, and gives life: He brings down to the grave, and brings up" (1 Sam. 2:6). Not only human life, but *life in general* is divine, is

---

5. Maimonides, *Hilkhot Rotzeah* 1:4: "For the soul of the one who was murdered is not the property of the blood avenger but of God."
6. "A man that is burdened with the blood of any person shall flee to the pit; let none support him" (Prov. 28:17), cited by Maimonides, *ibid.* 4:9.

held by God absolutely, and He is the only master who exercises unlimited dominion over it. Each life must be surrendered to God; this is the only way life shall be terminated. Destroying life because of selfish motives is forbidden. This applies to man and animal alike. With respect to human sacrifice, the religious ethos-experience interfered with the cult-experience and converted the actual sacrifice to a mental one, expressed in submission and surrender. Animal sacrifice, however, was retained by the Torah. The sacral act of offering a life to God is the only legitimate shedding of animal blood.

Killing an animal for the sake of satisfying my carnal desire – *besar ta'avah* – was classified as bloodshed and was therefore forbidden. Only after the people entered the Land of Israel did the Torah make a concession and begin to tolerate the slaughtering of animals for non-sacral purposes. To this compromise, however, many conditions were attached that make the slaughtering of the animal and its consumption the most complicated process. By committing the slightest error man may forfeit his privilege to enjoy the meat of the animal. But even as the Torah came to terms with the lusty sensual human being concerning the meat, it retained full possession and dominion over the blood. Blood is life, and as such it can never become the object of man's desire or lust – hence the many prohibitions against blood consumption (e.g., Lev. 17:11–12; Deut. 12:23). Blood shall be sacrificed to God on His altar, never misused by man for satisfying his carnal drives.

The Plant-Animal-Man Continuum

Sacrifices are drawn from the animal realm because the very idea of offering suggests the surrender of life to its rightful master, to God. But offerings are also drawn from the vegetable realm: wine, oil and flour take a most prominent place in the sacrificial lists. That all organic existence is on one continuum is a postulate of Judaism. But the Torah does not apply uniform standards to all organic life. Human life is evaluated as the apex of the bio-pyramid – what was termed *tzelem* – and plant as its base. But the difference consists only in degree, not in kind. Therefore all organic life was included in the sacral act of offering life to God.

The fact that the first budding of life must be consecrated to Him is a logical consequence of the idea that God is the rightful owner of all life. Every living creature owes its very existence to Him (in the simplest juridic meaning), and it is in the firstling that God's life-giving breath is most clearly manifest. The daybreak of life belongs to God, but is leased to man. As a result, Judaism proclaimed the idea of *bekhor*, the firstborn.

> Sanctify to Me all the firstborn, whatever opens the womb among the children of Israel, both of man and of beast, it is Mine (Ex. 13:2).

The firstborn shall be consecrated to God. The *bekhor* – man or animal – is claimed by the master. In the case of a clean animal, the firstborn is surrendered to God in the form of a sacrifice; in reference to humans and unclean animals, the Torah recommends redemption, a symbolic performance that still retains its aboriginal meaning in the formula which was composed by the Geonim: *"ma ba'it tefei?"* – "which do you prefer: to give away your firstborn son…or to redeem him…?"

It is critical that the idea that the *bekhor* belongs to God, expressing the unique intimacy between God and any living creature, includes vegetative life as well – *bikkurim*, first fruits.[7] Thus, Numbers mentions *bikkurim* together with the firstborn of man and animal (18:12–17).[8] *Terumah* (priestly due) and *hallah*

---

7. "Among the Hebrews, as among many other agricultural peoples, the offering of first-fruits was connected with the idea that it is not lawful or safe to eat of the new fruit until the god has received his due. The offering makes the whole crop lawful food." W. Robertson Smith, *Lectures on the Religion of the Semites. First Series: The Fundamental Institutions* (London: Adam and Charles Black, 1894), p. 241.

8. These verses deal with the idea that the first-created belong to God: the first-born, first-ripened, first-harvested, encompass human, animal and

(dough given to the priest) express the same idea; vegetative life, to be consumed by man, but first be consecrated to God, who is the source of all life.[9] In fact, the harvest is considered unfit for consumption (*tevel*) as long as the offering from that substance has not been given to the Lord. The logic is identical to that in regard to the slaughtering of animals in the desert: life – even of the plant – can only be claimed by God, and man has no right to destroy it. Of course, the Torah has granted man the privilege of using the plant, of destroying its life, only for his own sustenance. Yet it is only tenancy-rights that man holds in regard to vegetative life. It may never be acquired absolutely by him, an idea expressed regularly through *shemittah* (sabbatical year) and *yovel* (jubilee year): "...then shall the land keep a *Shabbat* to the Lord" (Lev. 25:2). God canceled man's specific rights and forbade him to exploit the soil and to reap its growth; God's rights are rehabilitated in the sabbatical years.

To sum up, in Judaism we cross the threshold of life upon entering the vegetative realm. Plant is a living creature and enjoys to a certain extent many prerogatives Judaism grants a being endowed with life. Sacrifices are limited to the animal and plant realms of life, for sacrifice means the return of life to its rightful owner. God does not lay any claim to inorganic, dead matter.[10] In

---

vegetative life, and are all God's possession (*herem*, objects dedicated to God, are included); He in turn transferred them to the *kohen*, the priest.

9. The prohibitions of *orlah* (fruit of the first three years of a tree's life) and *hadash* (eating of the new grain before the barley offering is brought in the Temple on Passover) bear evidence to the same concept. Man is not allowed to eat from the yield of the soil before he has brought the offering to God. The Halakhah extended the injunction of *hadash* to reaping; apparently, the only legitimate act of destruction consists in sacrificing life on the altar. For all life – human, animal and vegetative – belongs to God and must be surrendered to Him. In the act of sacrificing the first fruit, the earliest budding of life, God's mastery over and leadership of the world find expression.

10. The only exception to this rule is water, which is offered to God on the altar on Sukkot (*nissukh ha-mayim*). The reason for such a unique classification lies in the old Hebrew concept of *mayim hayyim* (lit. "living waters"),

the same vein, the Torah aimed at regulating only the interrelations between the human being and coexistent other living creatures since all of them are warmed by the divine breath. Inorganic matter is beyond the relational sphere. In order to establish any relational contact, a common ontic basis is necessary. No *issurim* (prohibitions) refer to inorganic things, for no relation exists between man and a dead world.

Here we grasp one of the most characteristic features of the Jewish anthropological philosophy. The deep feeling of man's basic harmony with organic nature – a harmony emerging from uniformity – is the most salient feature of that philosophical formula. Man may be the most developed form of life on the continuum of plant-animal-man, but the ontic essence remains identical.

---

i.e., that water is the very basis of all life. Though water itself is inorganic, it still conditions all kinds of living growth. Water is the springwell of life and is therefore symbolic of living matter. Once again, Judaism does not confine "life" solely to spiritual existence, but takes it in its aboriginal naturalistic meaning.

CHAPTER 3

Man and His Environment

In the first chapter, we identified the second characteristic of plant as its confluence with its environment. Let us therefore analyze man's confluence with his environment.

Prima facie, man and plant could not be more distinct. Plant is confined to its environment; man, in contrast, was endowed with the capacity of locomotion and this gift from heaven delivered him from eternal confinement. Nevertheless, if we view this in terms of affinity and integration with a specific milieu, man might indeed be like the plant. What is the attitude of Judaism concerning this problem? As always, it is necessary to examine a few Biblical texts and halakhic principles.

The Dynamic Nature of Divinity

Locomotion is one of the traits of life. This was known to both the Hebrew and the Greek of old. Plato considers the soul as the automotive principle. In speaking of God, the Bible never neglects to emphasize the dynamic aspect; God is identified with ceaseless movement, whether in the sense of continuous activity, like creation of, or eternal vigilance over, the universe, or locomotion. God comes and goes, visits the world and departs. The divine spirit is dynamic, restless.

> And *ruah E-lokim* [God's spirit or wind] moved over the surface of the water (Gen. 1:2).

Ruah denotes both spirit and wind for a simple reason: wind symbolizes motion, activity, speed – phenomena that are indispensable for a living being.

Fire and flame always accompany the revelation of God, whether at the burning bush, at the Sinaitic revelation, or the future Day of the Lord.[1] All are fire-apocalypses. "For the Lord your God is a consuming fire, a jealous God" (Deut. 4:26). Why? Fire has both a numinous aspect, symbolizing the destructiveness and remoteness of divinity that inspires grisly horror and shuddering, and a kinetic aspect, implying the activity and impetus of divinity. *Mobilitas Dei* is an important characteristic of the prophetic God.[2] God is eternal urgency and activity; He is compelling and alive. He comes and goes, descends and returns to His transcendent abode:

> Then the earth shook and trembled... There went up a smoke out of His nostrils, the fire out of His mouth devoured... He bowed the heavens also and came down; and darkness was under His feet. And He rode upon a cherub, and did fly: and He was seen (II Sam. 22:8–11).

The element of urgency, energy and kinesis is unique.

However, even divinity is "confined" to a specific locus. We cannot help but notice the intent of the Torah to "arrest" divinity within concrete bounds. The Sinaitic revelation demonstrated the inapproachability of God, His otherness and destructiveness on the one hand, and divine urgency and impetus on the other. Immediately thereafter, God commands Moses, "And let them

---

1. Exodus 3:2–3, 24:17; Joel 2:3, 3:3; Malachi 3:19.
2. It is interesting that in contrast to the prophetic God of *Tanakh*, both mystics and philosophers conceived of God in more static terms: either as an infinite all-pervading substance or as a life-inspiring universal soul. But both attempted to eliminate the kinetic moments from divinity. They saw in God absolute rest, peace and monotony. Indeed, they identified movement with the changeability and flow of time; the state of eternity requires immobility, rest and quietude.

make Me a Sanctuary; that I may dwell among them" (Ex. 25:8). Apparently, the Torah knew that while the dreadfulness and transcendental repulsion free divinity from all existing ties with this world, the moment of fascination and attractiveness tries to achieve almost the impossible – to introduce God into a concrete confine or abode. There is a definite tendency to imprison the infinite, transcendental deity within the bounds of our concrete universe. The source of this concept is Ezekiel's famous epiphany: *barukh kevod Hashem mi-mekomo* (3:12) – God has a *makom*, a place. God imposes voluntary imprisonment on Himself, by His own free will arrests Himself within the confines of a cosmic order in general, and within a hallowed abode in particular. Solomon asked this impertinent question:

> Then spoke Solomon: "The Lord said that He would dwell in the thick darkness. I have surely built You a house to dwell in, a settled place for You to abide in forever.... For will God indeed dwell on the earth? Behold the heavens, and heaven of heavens cannot contain You; how much less this house which I have built" (1 Kings 8:12–13, 26).

In this wonderful prayer, Solomon formulated the most paradoxical mystery of divinity. Infinity and universality on the one hand, and self-contraction on the other; freedom and continuous movement under one aspect, confinement within certain bounds, under another. The Midrash relates the same paradox in different words:

> At the time God said to Moses "Build Me a *mishkan* [Tabernacle]," Moses began to wonder, saying: "God's glory fills the upper and lower worlds, and He tells me 'Build Me a *mishkan*'!? Therefore, Moses said: "He who dwells in the secret place of the most high shall abide under the shadow of the Almighty" (Ps. 91:1). Said God: "I do not think as you do. Rather, twenty boards on the north, twenty on the south, eight in the west [are sufficient to contain Me]; not only that,

> but I will descend and contract my Presence within [the space
> of] a square cubit" (*Num. Rabbah* 12:3).

Moses could not reconcile God's transcendence with self-limita-
tion, "He who dwells in the sacred place of the most high shall
abide under the shadow of the Almighty" with "I shall dwell in
their midst" (Ex. 25:8). According to the Midrash, God revealed
to him the mystery of *tzimtzum* ("contraction"). Apparently, life is
expressed in the polarity of freedom and confinement, continuous
movement and arrest within a bounded environment. It applies
equally to both God and man.

Thus, human life is not only movement; it is also imprisonment within and integration with a stable frame of reference. A
man is not allowed to tear away from his natural moorings; in
this respect, he is more like plant than animal. He takes root, he
is stationary and forms one entity with his environment. And like
plant, that environment is the soil: both belong to Mother Earth,
and both are part of her.

Man's Relationship with the Earth

At this point, we may examine the unique relationship that prevails between man and earth.

First, the earth claims man; he was taken out of Mother Earth,
and to her he must return.

> ... until you return to the ground; for out of it you were taken:
> for dust you are, and to dust shall you return (Gen. 3:19).

The *mitzvah* of burial indicates the validity of the demand the
earth makes on man. She insists upon the return of a part of her
own self. As soon as the *ruah E-lokim* departs man, his inanimate
body must be delivered to its rightful owner.

Let us penetrate more deeply into this mysterious man-earth
relationship. God put primordial man in paradise for the specific
purpose of tilling and keeping it:

> And the Lord God took the man, and put him into the Garden of Eden to till it and to keep it (Gen. 2:15).

Obviously the prime task of man was to cultivate the ground:

> And no plant of the field was yet in the earth, and no herb of the field had yet grown: for the Lord God had not caused it to rain upon the earth, and there was not a man to till the earth (Gen. 2:5)

The close, intimate association between man and earth is already formulated in unequivocal words. The earth serves man; as long as there was no man, vegetative life did not emerge. On the other hand, man serves the earth; he is her servant and slave. *La-avod* is the term for "service";[3] the expressions *la-avod et ha-adamah* and *le-ovdah u-le-shomrah* both mean "to serve the earth." Paradoxically, man both serves Mother Earth and subdues her (Gen. 1:28). Apparently there prevails harmony between Mother Earth and her children. They both need each other. There is cooperation and accord. Why? Because man was created out of the earth; there was a common ontic basis of man's existence and nature-reality. There was correspondence, mutual response and cooperation.

Yet this state of peace and harmony did not last long. Paradisical man enjoyed the friendship and good will of his Mother-Earth. The first sin disturbed this beautiful harmony. Man sinned in the paradise and betrayed nature. We do not know at this point the nature of that sin, whether it was rebellion, concupiscence or ignorance. We do know, however, that harmony was transformed into tension, concord into conflict, and coexistence into divided existences.

---

3. The same term applies to divine service: "What mean you by this service?" (Ex. 12:26); "And you shall serve the Lord your God" (Ex. 23:25); "But the Levites shall do the service" (Num. 18:23); "And to serve Him with all your heart" (Deut. 11:13).

> And to the man He said, "Because you have hearkened to
> the voice of your wife, and have eaten of the tree, of which I
> commanded you, saying, 'You shall not eat of it': cursed be
> the ground for your sake; in sorrow shall you eat of it all the
> days of your life; thorns and thistles shall it bring forth to
> you; and you shall eat the herb of the field. In the sweat of
> your face you shall eat bread, till you return to the ground;
> for out of it was you taken: for dust you are, and to dust you
> shall return" (Gen. 3:17–20).

The earth was burdened with a curse *ba-avurekha*, "because of your
deed." You defiled the soil, you contaminated her. The latter ceased
to be responsive to man's needs. "Work" no longer describes a cooperative effort on the part of man and nature; it is now a struggle
with nature, a mutual dislike. Man eats the fruits of Mother Earth
in sorrow and by the sweat of his brow. The mother suddenly has
become a stepmother, indifferent to man's pains and sufferings, at
times even malicious. "Thorns and thistles shall it bring forth to
you." Nature does not trust man any more; she hates to feed him
or comply with his desires. Now man begins to fight nature, to
conquer her by stealing her secrets, by spying on her, by compelling
her into submission. The struggle is long, tedious and exhausting.
In other words, man confronts nature in a hostile, fighting mood.

When Cain committed the first crime of fratricide, the antagonism between man and earth deepened; the conflict became
even more bitter than before:

> When you till the ground, it shall henceforth not yield unto
> you her strength, a fugitive and vagabond shall you be in the
> earth (Gen. 4:12).

While paradisical man could at least obtain some beneficial results
from his hard work, Cain was condemned to both unproductive
toil and continual wandering. The earth rejected him fully; she
refused him even shelter and refuge.

Mother Earth reacts to sin, she condemns the sinner doggedly and ruthlessly. She is very sensitive to moral wrong.

> You shall not lie with a man after the manner of a woman, it is abomination. Neither shall you lie with any beast to defile yourself with it; neither shall any woman stand before a beast to lie down before it, it is perversion. Defile not yourselves in any of these cases... and the land was defiled: therefore I do punish its iniquity upon it, and the land vomits out its inhabitants (Lev. 18:22–25).

> So you shall not pollute the land in which you are, for blood pollutes the land, and the land cannot be cleansed of the blood that is shed therein, but by the blood of him that shed it. And you shall not defile the land which you shall inhabit, in which I dwell: for I the Lord dwell among the children of Israel (Num. 35:33–34)

Sin defiles not only human beings, but the earth as well. The earth becomes desecrated, polluted by crime, and needs absolution or atonement. In the case of murder, the atonement can be made to the land only by the blood of the murderer; in that of illicit sexual relations, by casting out the sinner.

It is indeed unique to speak of *tum'ah* (ritual impurity) as attached to Mother Earth. A metaphysical quality is ascribed to her. Sin and atonement apply to both man and earth. Why? Because man is a part of her, man is nature expressed in a meaningful existence. He can never, however, free himself from that union. Earth, nature and man flow into each other. There is complete identity of man and earth. Let us not forget that by the word "earth", we understand not just the land but nature as a whole, the entire complex of physical conditions that make man's existence possible. As an organism, he depends upon his surroundings, and this dependence spells ontic unity and uniformity. Obedience to God means "Then I will give you rain in due season, and the land shall yield her increase, and the trees of the field shall yield their fruit"; disobedience – "...and I will make your skies like iron, and your earth like brass, and your strength shall be spent in vain, for your land shall not yield her increase, neither shall the trees of the land yield their fruit" (Lev. 26:4, 19–20).

When a community refuses to live in accordance with the divine law, Mother Nature becomes non-cooperative, refusing to subordinate herself to man's rule. With sin, the gap widens. Nature begins to resent the presence of man; in response, man attempts to subjugate an insurgent and malicious nature. The struggle, once begun, ends in man's defeat. Mother earth spits out her unruly son. Man is cast out of his environment.

> When you shall beget children, and children's children, and you shall have remained long in the land, and shall deal corruptly, and make a carved idol...I call heaven and earth to witness against you this day, that you shall soon utterly perish from off the land into which you go over the Jordan to possess it (Deut. 4:25–26).

The most typical punishment in the Bible – to paradisaical man, to Cain, to the Jewish people – is exile, being cast out not by society but by nature. Mother Earth is unwilling to grant man shelter and refuge.

What does all this mean?

First, there is a very close kinship between man and nature. Nature, when confined within the God-intended scheme of things, is perfect. The same applies to man. As long as man lives within the bounds set by his Creator, which accentuate his naturalness, he remains *ben adam*, the son of Mother Earth, and may claim asylum in her lap. When nature showers man with generosity and kindness, she is kind to herself, to her son who is an integral part of her, bone of her bones and flesh of her flesh. As long as man lives in unison with natural law, he remains protected from the defilement of sin.

But when he begins to sin, to grasp for something not belonging to him, he divorces himself from a natural existence, from that finite and determinate character of an earthly being. And this spells doom for man. Sin is *hamas*; as we proved in a previous chapter, *hamas* means deterioration in the sense of unnaturalness, in reaching beyond one's own possibilities and opportunities. And man is defiled by sin – it produces *tum'ah* (defilement). *Tum'ah* is identical with death or disease: hence it is associated with *met* (corpse), *nevelah* (carrion), *sheretz* (creeping swarming thing), *zav, zavah, metzora* and *yoledet*. All these are anomalous in organic life; pathology is identical with *tum'ah*.

What is true of physical *tum'ah* is true as well for spiritual *tum'ah, tum'at ha-het* (defilement from sin). Any anomaly in the pattern of living, any pathological deviation from the straight path of existence, is *tum'ah*. Let us not forget that the Hebrew word for transgression, *avon*, comes from the root *ivah*, to distort or twist. *Het*, sin, means not to live in full compliance with the natural designs embedded in my existence by God. While Christianity kept on preaching that sin means surrender to nature and rebellion against God,[4] Judaism stated the total opposite: Sin is detachment from nature and non-compliance with her dicta. (It is no accident that the term *tum'ah* was used by the Bible exclusively in regard to adultery, murder and idolatry, which are considered unnatural sins. The injunction against such offenses binds every human being, not just Jews.) Man's involvement in a natural existence is recommended, whereas his estrangement from nature is branded as sin. Man becomes corrupt when he acts in an unnatural way, not fitting his natural existence. Unnaturalness equals *hamas*.

What is the consequence of this *tum'ah*? As soon as man

---

4. "But men, having rejected things eternal, and, by the counsel of the devil, turned to the things of corruption, became the cause of their own corruption in death; being, as I said before, by nature corruptible, but destined, by the grace following from partaking of the Word, to have escaped their natural state, had they remained perfect." Athanasius of Alexandria (4th cent.), *On the Incarnation of the Word* 5:1.

begins to act in a manner alien to his nature, as soon as he tries to transcend nature's limitations and bounds, she changes her attitude toward him. He has expressed contempt and disdain for his Mother Earth; nature on her part refuses to promote man's interests, which are not hers any more.

We may conclude from these premises the following:

(1) The metaphysical confluence of man and nature is a postulate of Judaism.

(2) This coexistence results in co-responsibility. This is both negative and positive: man's sin as well as his good deeds are also nature's. Man can either corrupt and defile nature or sanctify her. In case of good, Mother Earth is credited together with man, and shares her blessing with him; in the case of man's sin, the earth is defiled, and bears the brunt of his crimes. In order to free herself from the indictment, she must denounce man, dissolve the ties prevailing between them. Mother Earth has no choice; otherwise she will be branded a criminal.

> Do not prostitute your daughter, to cause her to be a harlot, lest the land fall to harlotry, and the land become full of harlotry (Lev. 19:29).

> And the land was defiled, therefore I do punish its iniquity upon it (18:25).

The earth falls to whoredom, the earth becomes defiled, the earth is punished for man's sins. The only alternative is to renounce her association with man and cast him out: "...and the land vomits out her inhabitants" (Lev. 18:25).

The same is true of murder, deliberate or unintentional:

> And now cursed are you from the earth, which has opened its mouth to receive your brother's blood from your hand (Gen. 4:11).

> So you shall not pollute the land in which you are, for blood pollutes the land, and the land cannot be cleansed of the blood that is shed therein, but by the blood of him that shed it (Num. 35:33).

Through man's sin, the land becomes polluted and defiled, and needs atonement. When man is cursed, Mother Earth herself is indicted together with him.

In sum, the blessings and curses of Leviticus 26 do not constitute a promise of reward or punishment, but a statement of a fact – man's confluence with nature.

(3) Thus, man is not a universal abstract being who roams along the infinite lanes of the cosmos without finding attachment to any part of it. He is confined to a determinate finite world; he must, like the plant, be rooted in an enclosed part of the soil and live together with nature. For man, therefore, the greatest curse is to wander from place to place, unable to take root anywhere. The curse of Cain was: "a fugitive and a vagabond shall you be on the earth" (Gen. 4:12).

Man's Stewardship of Mother Earth

At this point, it is fair to raise what to many will be on obvious question: is not the notion of man's partnership with Mother Earth at odds with the Biblical notion of man's dominion over nature?

> ...replenish the earth, and subdue it: and have dominion over the fish of the sea, and over the birds of the air...(Gen. 1:28).

> You makest him to have dominion over the works of Your hands; You have put all things under his feet: all sheep, and oxen, and also the beasts of the field; the birds of the sky, and the fish of the seas, whatever passes through the paths of the seas (Ps. 8:7–9).

How is the rule of man over nature warranted if man is nothing but a son of Mother Earth? The answer to this problem is very simple. Man's dominion of nature is *not* that of an alien autocrat over a people subjugated by force, but that of a loving father over his young son, or of a devoted son over an incapacitated old mother. Nature surrenders voluntarily to man's control and rule, she entrusts man with her most guarded secrets. It is more cooperation than dominion, more partnership than subordination. Let us watch out for moments of tension and conflict, when nature begins to hate man and to resent his presence, and we will convince ourselves that man's sense of security and strength is nothing but a mirage. If nature refuses to be dominated, man is left helpless and weak. There is some sort of covenant between man and nature. The prime condition of such a contractual relationship is man's living up to certain natural standards. By the slightest error, man forfeits his rights to dominate and becomes an outcast. This is man's freedom: either to live at peace with nature and thus give expression to a natural existence in the noblest of terms, or to surpass his archaic bounds and corrupt himself and nature. Man's freedom is embedded in his confinement to his environment, in his coexistence with nature. This vision of man may externally resemble that of the naturalists, but is profoundly different in inner significance. According also to modern naturalistic philosophers, man's identity with nature is certain; his existence is a natural existence. But they deny man's freedom to ennoble or to defile nature. For them the contact is stable. Judaism understands an intelligent relationship that fluctuates between full harmony and antagonism.

But does not the concept of *tzelem E-lokim* denote a new transcendental addendum to the human being, one that is nonexistent in nature? Let us not forget that God is seen under two aspects: (1) under that of transcendence and infinity; (2) under that of immanence and confinement. *Tzelem E-lokim* refers exactly to the second aspect. God is confined within the cosmos, present in His creation, and only because of His presence, He guides and rules the cosmos. Similarly, man dominates his environment; his oneness with the outside world enables him to rule it. Were he transcendent, he could not adapt himself to the world.[5]

In the following chapter, we shall deal with the problem of man's superiority. What is important to emphasize now is the fact that man is confined to a specific area in the cosmos and his task is to live in full harmony with his environment. Nor is this environment totally static. At times, it is determined by certain historical events. Like man, it emerges through the historical process. The Bible usually defined this unique environment in terms of man meeting God. Man, in his confinement, and God, in His voluntary exile, meet at certain crossroads. God chances upon and surprises man. By virtue of this sudden encounter, man takes root in this mystical place. Jacob met God in Beit-El and a new bond between him and that place formed.

> I am the God of Beit-El, where you did anoint a pillar, and where you did vow a vow to Me: now arise, get out of this land, and return to the land of your birth (Gen. 31:13).

The union of God-man-place is expressed here. Jacob was imprisoned within a geographic area, but together with him, God confined Himself to that place.

This paradigm is crucial to understanding Judaism: as a natural being, man is arrested within concreteness and, as such, can never reach a transcendent God. In order to meet man (i.e., revelation), God descends from transcendental infinity into concrete

---

5. In the same way, the epistemological problem that baffled the minds of the greatest philosophers finds its solution in the communion of man with nature. "How is pure mathematics possible?" asked Kant. In other words, how can mathematical principles that were conceived by man in his seclusion from nature (a priori) be applied to the chaotic manifold of reality? Apparently man is equipped with a faculty of divination. Because of his kinship with the cosmos, he reads the inner workings of nature. It is impossible to abstract man from his natural background.

finitude and confines Himself to the identical area in which man was placed. Man discovers God within finitude, within man's own realm, and this discovery determines man's belonging to a determinate environment. *Kedushah* (holiness) bespeaks God's and man's entirety, a definite segment of the cosmos and their encounter there. When man frees himself from such natural bonds, he loses contact with his God.

The historical curse of *galut*, of exile, appears to express this tragedy of full freedom, of losing the man-plant trait of communion with the outside. Particularly, man-plant is incapable of meeting his destiny as an uprooted, abstract spiritual being, not having any bonds with primordial Mother Earth. God, confined *kivyakhol* (as it were) within the cosmos, wants man to be confined. Statehood, or redemption, embodies the return to the primordial man-locus union. This is the rebirth of a man both free and confined, whose task is to redeem nature by living in unison with her dictates and designs. The state cannot be reduced to social interrelationships alone, but must be extended to the mystical communion of man with nature, the renewal of an old friendship, a reconciliation between man and Mother Earth. The state commits man to the soil, to nature, chains him to a bounded specific environment, enabling him to take root in an ancient soil out of which the primitive clan emerged, and within whose confines he experienced the unusual encounter with God.

The state is charged not only with ennobling man in his relationship to others, but mainly with establishing an ideal continuation between man and nature. The former has duties, obligations not only toward his fellow man but toward nature. They coexist, are co-responsible; nature bears the blame for man's deeds. If man sins, nature pays the penalty and is cursed; if he lives a normal life, nature is invigorated, and both are blessed. Man is a creative being in reference to nature. In cultivation of the soil, in scientific discovery, in all manner of creative work man cooperates with nature, sows and worships her. God Himself *kivyakhol* has not found a more important occupation than farming: "And the Lord God planted a garden eastward in Eden..." (Gen. 2:8).

It is imperative for man to plant and cultivate the ground:

Six years you shall sow the land, and shall gather in its fruits (Ex. 23:10).

When you come into the land, you shall plant all manner of trees for food (Lev. 19:23).

Man *should* create new life; he *should* plant trees and engage in such creative work. The intimate close contact with the environment was recommended and approved by Judaism. The Jew whom God called upon was a worker, a farmer, a shepherd; men who lived in harmony and at peace with nature and saw God not in transcendent heavens, but descending from infinity into finitude. They had spoken to Him as to their fellow-men, in a friendly, neighborly fashion. To cultivate the ground means to worship: *avodah*. In it is expressed man's loyalty to himself and to his destiny.

CHAPTER 4

Man as Animal and the Emergence
of the Ethical Norm

The Halakhah was well aware that biologically and physiologically, there is little difference between man and animal. Medical research is based upon the similarity of both concerning all organic pathological phenomena. In the same way, the concept of *terefah*, which denotes any organic anomaly (structural and functional), refers to animal and man alike.[1] The prophets used the *adam u-behemah* (man-animal) analogy quite often, although admittedly not to the extent they availed themselves of the parable of man-plant.

He is like the beasts that perish (Ps. 49:13).

And make men like the fishes of the sea (Hab. 1:14).

O Lord, You preserve man and beast (Ps. 36:7).

---

1. Maimonides discriminated between animal and human *terefah* insofar as he described *terefot* of animals in fixed halakhic terms that are valid independently of the progress of medical science and *terefot* of the human in a strict medical fashion. *Terefot* of humans he defined as any malady that afflicts human beings and which is, in the opinion of the physicians, incurable. Cf. *Hilkhot Shehitah* 10:9 and *Hilkhot Rotzeah* 2:8.

However, we are not at this moment interested in man as compared with animal in terms of complex tissue systems or biochemical tendencies, like the reaction of the body to temperature, to oxygen or food concentration, and similar metabolic processes. Instead we would like to analyze the halakhic viewpoint of man-animal in regard to biological-psychical motivation and drives; in other words, processes associated with a conscious *act*.

There are many biochemical activities that do not involve any psychical aspects. For instance, no specific pattern of external behavior is required of animal and man in connection with biochemical assimilation processes. The organism performs its task in deep slumber. The term "activity" itself in this context is not exact: activity denotes only specific changes that follow a steady, uniform pattern. It would, however, be nonsensical to apply the word "activity" in the sense of *act*, a deed that is equipped with directedness and necessary meaning. In other words, the behavior is completely concentrated on the physical-chemical level. No sensory psychical components are involved.

There are, in contrast, cases where the biochemical organism as such cannot satisfy its own needs. It must call upon the animal, the living creature, for assistance. The organism cannot act exclusively through the biochemical medium of tissue behavior, but is forced to mobilize its psychical dynamics, which overlap its physical activity. For instance, under the stress of the hunger drive, the animal will look for food. In the same way, the sexual need will periodically impel the creature to behave in a specific fashion which will ultimately lead to the act of mating. This type of instinctive drive – a push or, as Bergson liked to call it, *élan* – is an *act*, in the sense that the living creature, determined by visceral and sensory drives, submits itself to the insistence of its own organism. There is, however, a distinct *act*, which can epistemologically be separated from the drive.

Features of Instinctive Behavior

This instinctive behavior is usually characterized by four basic traits:[2]

(1) Automatic behavior, although motivated by biological stress, displays directedness. Thus the moth follows a beautifully definite curve of orientation toward a source of light. The movements are not only stimulated by, but directed upon, a specific object, namely the light. The animal may act under blind pressure directed upon it, but we cannot help saying that the animal is *motivated* in doing so, in not acting in any other way. There is semantic conditioning of such activity; it is endowed with meaning that does not belong to the sphere of intelligent awareness.

(2) In contrast with logical human anticipation, which precedes a deliberate act, instinctive behavior displays an inseparable unity of objectives and acting. When the birds fly southward, we get the impression that the bird is striving for a certain objective and is "aware" of its existence, on one hand, and of the means that lead to its attainment, on the other. The animal "expects" some new situations and gets ready for an emergency that does not yet exist. The bird leaves the northern climate for the sunny south; the bear prepares its lodgings for the winter, and so on. The behavior of the animal attests to some instinctive push in regard to a future exigency. The biological-psychical expectancy is not the forerunner of, but a concomitant to, the instinctive performance. It is not as if the bird becomes agitated in the late summer because it foresaw this cold spell and the uneasiness impelled the creature to start out for the south. Nothing of the sort occurs. The biological push brings about simultaneously both the "instinctive" prescience and performance.

(3) The fields of both biology and psychology accept that the instinct is the means by which the survival of the *species* is made

---

2.   Gardner Murphy, *Personality: A Biosocial Approach to Origins and Structure* (New York: Harper & Brothers, 1947), pp. 92 ff.

possible.[3] Instinctive behavior is not directed upon the survival of the individual; indeed, the individual will many a time expose itself to discomfort and even danger in order to carry out some kind of task that the instinct has imposed upon him and which in the long run serves the interests of the species. In other words, the "principle of sacrifice" – security of the species – is the guiding motif of instinctive performance.

(4) In seeking satisfaction, the instinctive motivation is oriented toward a multitude of objectives, without the organism discriminating between one objective and another. While on its original, natural path, the primordial drive is uniform and all-inclusive with respect to the organism's biological demands; it neither focuses its pressure upon specific objects nor prioritizes some needs at the expense of others. The sexual tensions, the hunger-drive, the impulse for movement, and so on, are all equally appreciated by the aboriginal instinct and equally discharged. Moreover, the biological drive disregards the attendant circumstances of its consummation. Whether the performance is accompanied by pleasure or not is impertinent to the innate impulse. Only upon repeated experience, and with learning, does the drive begin to operate according to the criterion of selectivity, both in terms of specific objects and with respect to particular drives.[4] After this, we may say that the biological energies yearning for an outlet break through the barrier at a given spot, channeled into a drive that is selective and discriminating. But this process

---

3. Jean-Henri Fabre, in his stupendous work *Souvenirs Entomologiques* on the lives and manners of insects, proved beyond any reasonable doubt that primordial instinctive behavior differs from that acquired by self-training (guided by the principle of trial and error) insofar as the former displays servility to the species as a whole, while the latter occupies itself with the individual.

4. According to Murphy, only after these repeated experiences do "the general motives (which are at first rather non-specifically related to a class of stimuli) tend to become more easily satisfied through the action of a specific satisfier than of others of the same general class" (p. 162). Murphy calls this process "canalization," a term he borrows from Janet.

emerges into the biological arena at a later phase. In the course of this growing selectivity, the animal becomes aware of its own individual insistences and directs its energies toward a preferred objective. In other words, instead of guarding the species, the animal begins to protect (truly or falsely) its *own* interests. Gradually, the element of treachery begins to appear on the surface of instinctive behavior. Learning by associative memory – a feature of mammals more than of any other class of species – makes the animal a traitor to the group, to the species. The dog or the ape is "pleasure seeking" and dominated by "hedonic motives"; the individual animal begins to detach itself from the group and to adapt its drives to its own unique needs and demands. Constant repetition and accumulation of "experience" pave the paths into which the discharge of the unique biological energies will be channeled.

The selection of those paths, of those methods that realize the instinctive drive, serves a twofold purpose: (1) a successful performance; (2) a pleasant performance. Through trial and error, both animal and man find out the how and the what: how to perform their task in the most successful way and what amount of pleasure to expect from such a performance. In other words, the technological ability and hedonic addiction are results of the mechanization of primordial biological drives. Both are the font of creativity and uniqueness. They free the individual from his servitude to the species.

But there is also a risk, for when the original drive is freed from its naturalness and dedication to its original task, it may become a negative factor in the life of the species and the individual. Excessive indulgence in and repetition of a particular instinctive activity because of its concomitant hedonic moments leads to biological and psychological anomalies. The instinctive drive directed by a mechanized associative memory and technical intelligence may turn into a fiend of human and animal life.

Man as Animal in the Perspective of Judaism

Let us now examine all those aspects in the light of Judaism by turning to the story of man as related in Genesis.

> And God said, "Let us make mankind in our image, after our likeness: and let them have dominion over the fish of the sea, and over the birds of the air, and over the cattle, and over all the earth, and over every creeping thing that creeps on the earth." So God created mankind in His own image, in the image of God He created him; male and female He created them. And God blessed them, and God said to them, "Be fruitful and multiply, replenish the earth and subdue it: and have dominion over the fish of the sea, and over the birds of the air, and over every living thing that moves on the earth." And God said, "Behold, I have given you every herb bearing seed, which is upon the face of all the earth . . . to you it shall be for food. And to every beast of the earth, and to every bird of the air, and to everything that creeps on the earth, wherein there is life. I have given every green herb for food": and it was so (Gen. 1:26–30).

Comparing the blessing given to man with the one given to animal –

> And God blessed them, saying, "Be fruitful and multiply, and fill the waters in the seas, and let birds multiply in the earth" (Gen. 1:22) –

we notice both similarities and discrepancies. Both species are commanded *peru u-revu* – "be fruitful and multiply." We must understand this blessing of multiplication, uttered at the creation of animal and man but absent at the creation of vegetative life, to be the instinctive drive that finds expression in a directed act. The unique property of the animal in contradistinction to the plant asserts itself not in the biochemical capacity for regeneration, which

70

is a trait common to both,[5] but in the biological motivation of and push toward the same *act* of procreation. While in the vegetative realm fruition is carried out by itself – it is done without having a doer become active – the animal acts (of course instinctively) in order that multiplication be attained. In other words, the *regionalized* biochemical insistence of the organism employs the help of the *whole* animal, who must perform an act to satisfy the drive. That instinctive drive to multiplication, synonymous with sexual hunger and tension, was God's blessing to the zoological realm. That is why "blessing," in the Biblical context, is always associated with the grammatical imperative: it singles out an act on the part of the organism, an act that is both directed (i.e., meaningful) and generic.

The objective of copulation in both animals and humans is the need for expansion and multiplication of the species and genera:

> ...and fill the waters in the seas, and let birds multiply in the earth (1:22).

The individual animal is stimulated by biochemical energies, and responds in a peculiar fashion in the form of directed performance – all to perpetuate the life of the species. If we look closely at the verses of the fifth and sixth days, we are amazed at the emphasis placed on genus and species in the organic realm.

> ...and let "birds" [lit., "the bird"] multiply in the earth (1:22).

> ...and every living creature that moves...*after their kind*, and every winged bird *of its kind*...(1:21)

---

5.   "Let the earth bring forth grass, herb yielding seed and fruit tree yielding fruit after its kind whose seed is in itself" (Gen. 1:11) applies to plant and animal alike.

And God made the beasts [lit., "the beast"] of the earth *after their kind*, and cattle after their kind, and everything that creeps on the earth *after its kind* (1:25).

The species conditions the biological motivation. The individual constitutes only a medium, through which the morphological development of the species is realized.

As with animals, the blessing of "be fruitful and multiply" to man implies not only the organic capacity for regeneration but the biological impulse and movement toward it. But we do notice a slight difference in man's blessing: the ultimate objective of that drive is not expansion of the species or genus but dominion over nature.

...replenish the earth, and subdue it: and have dominion over the fish of the sea (1:28).

In contrast to the animals, man's rule over nature forms an integral part of his biological push toward expansion and multiplication. The Torah has interwoven his drive for power with that of *peru u-revu*. The difference between man and animal as to their biological motivation is not very fundamental: it is only a difference as to the degree of zoological expansion, not as to the kind. Whereas for the animal, expansion does not imply dominion over other species, for man both attributes are combined: by expanding he attains power and dominion over other species.

The reason for this peculiar combination, of expansion turning into dominion, is to be found in the ability of man to develop his biological drive into technical intelligence, which is guided by the associative memory. The know-how is by far more pronounced in man than in animal. The technological capacity, although not constituting a unique endowment of man, is nevertheless more developed in him than in the animal. It is again a gradual difference, yet a very important one. The main distinction lies in the fact that while man projects his accumulated experience onto the past and thus frees his associative capacity for a never-ceasing process of learning and anticipating and experiencing the unknown, the animal, not apprehending time in its two-directional expansion, neither relates its experience to the past nor anticipates the infinite character of experience.

The immediate conclusion that we may derive from such considerations is twofold: (1) Human personality (*tzelem*) is motivated and ruled by the instinctive drive, but it attains perfection in the form of technical intelligence which appoints man as the ruler of other living species. In the words of the psalmist: "You make him to have dominion over the work of your hands; you have put all things under his feet" (8:7). (2) Such a biological-psychical capacity was created and sanctioned by God. The divine approval of the biological impulse is repeated in the Torah twice: once at the beginning of the sixth day (1:25), in sole reference to the zoological realm, and once at the end of the same day (1:31), in reference as well to man. When we take into account that God also sanctioned the biochemical insistences of organic matter as such when vegetation sprung into existence on the third day (1:12), the net result is that man is good under all three aspects: (1) as a biochemical organism (plant) endowed with all the organic insistences and propensities; (2) as an animal with all his automatic, primordial, biological act dynamics (the sexual drive, the appetite); (3) as a man-animal who brought his biological motivation to perfection and converted it to a technical intelligence which guides man in his execution of the biological drive. It is at this point that Judaism breaks with Christianity. Christianity has been bent upon a transcendental adventure, namely, to free man from his bondage to the flesh and raise him to a spiritual level. Judaism, in contrast, proclaimed the goodness of the whole of man, of the natural man-plant-animal.

Man as Distinct from Animal

We have thus far analyzed two aspects, two layers in the human being: non-directed biochemical-plant-existence; and natural dynamic animal-existence guided by a technical intelligence. However, the community and equality of man and animal comes to an end at this point. Reading the story of man carefully, we notice that the Torah used a unique term in regard to him. While the divine blessing to animal is described as *va-yevarekh otam E-lokim* (God blessed them), in the blessing to man a new term was introduced, namely, *va-yomer lahem* (He said to them).

> And God blessed them and God said them, "Be fruitful and multiply" (1:28).

The simple word *va-yomer* (He said) sheds a new light upon man, and upon his role and task. *Va-yevarekh* (He blessed) denotes the embedding into the organic frame of existence its specific tensions and insistences, by which the animal is driven to a certain performance. The *va-yevarekh* does not constitute any norm or ethical law. But in the case of man, God also spoke to him. He informed him of his biological propensities and tendencies. Through His speech to man, God registered in the latter's mind the necessity of this automatic drive, thus transforming it into a conscious, deliberate, anticipated act, directed upon the same objective. The automatic push and blind, forced movement of *va-yevarekh* turn into a conscious drive and intelligent movement of *va-yomer*.[6] In contrast to animals, man yields to his natural instinct not only because he is driven by biochemical forces to such behavior but also because he is motivated. Through *va-yomer*, biological mechanical drives and teleological intelligent motifs are interwoven.

The consequence of such a premise is enormous. Man's natural existence is good not only because of a negative reason (it is not corrupt) but mainly because it is a *planned* existence. To exist

---

6. To be sure, the word *va-yomer* does appear in the earlier days of creation, but these denote only the act of creation. God did not speak to any created object. Only in the case of man was *va-yomer* grammatically combined with the indirect object, *lahem* (to them).

fully in unison with all biological insistences and tensions means to exist intelligently.

This identity of biological impulse and ethical motivation is quite conspicuous in the second *va-yomer* announced to man:

> And God said, "Behold, I have given you every herb bearing seed, which is upon the face of all the earth, and every tree, on which is the fruit yielding seed, for you it shall be for food" (Gen. 1:29).

Man was confined to the yield of the soil. Only cereal food was assigned to him. He was not allowed to kill any living creature. As we have indicated above, this injunction against a carnivorous life includes both a natural aversion to flesh *and* an ethical norm. At this crossroads, animal and man part. The former remains arrested within biological automatism, the latter experiences it on a higher plane – as an ethical opportunity.

Moreover, according to the Biblical story, man acquires biological awareness of himself. By the mere fact that he was confronted by God and spoken unto, the I-thou relationship emerges. The thou makes the I self-conscious; he comes in contact with the other one. The knowledge of otherness makes him aware of his ego existence. Yet in this case, the thou is not a being similar to him, but God Himself.

This, then, is the third, and distinct, aspect of man from the rest of creation: existence filled with ethical meaning. To be sure, even under this third aspect, man is not necessarily charged with specific new tasks. He is enriched only by a new modality, which adds a new quality to his existence. Temporarily the Torah has limited the ethical norm to the biological push.

Tzelem E-lokim: The Divine Image

It is here that the notion of *tzelem E-lokim* makes its first appearance. Under the aspect of *va-yomer lahem E-lokim* ("and the Lord spoke to them"), *tzelem* signifies man's awareness of himself as a biological being and the state of being informed of his natural drives. It implies foreknowledge of man's own pressures and instinctive tendencies, and of the necessity of complying with the insistence of the organism. At this point again Judaism differs from Christianity. Christianity viewed instinct as corrupt and sinful; man's divine essence asserts itself in his spirit, which is always in a state of war with the flesh. Judaism rehabilitates the flesh by offering it the attribute of *tzelem*, attaching the quality of divine image to the biological forces in man.

However, we must proceed very cautiously in formulating this *tzelem* element. At this point of the creation story, it is still premature to import the ethical law into man's existential state. The *va-yomer lahem E-lokim* is still arrested within natural objective bounds, with nature as it exists in its immediate, instinctive, but organically uniform and "unbroken" course of the life functions. The God who addresses Himself to man, who blesses him and informs him of his bonds with Mother Nature, is *E-lokim*, God as revealed in the cosmic process, in the regularity, unity and continuity of the same. *E-lokim* is the fountainhead of cosmic dynamics: a prime mover, a creator, an engineer, yet an impersonal being. As yet, God Himself had not appeared as a *personality* – and therefore man could not conceive of himself as a person. Adam is still an animal crawling in the jungle, still the ape which is aware of its needs. Man may have acquired a technical intelligence that makes tools and organizes, but his awareness was utilitarian, technical. He possessed the ability of selecting the media that guaranteed a successful performance by the instinct. The specific human element – the moral "agent" – had not yet come to birth. Unique ethical norms were, as yet, impossible.

The Emergence of the Ethical Norm

What exactly are the prerequisites for the emergence of the ethical norm? We can delineate three stages through which man becomes aware of himself as an ethical being:

(1) An act is ethical when it is sponsored by two motives: the *imperativistic*, that is, under the pressure of a normative feeling; and the *idealistic*, namely, the fulfillment of the norm is experienced as redeeming, elevating and meaning-giving. The ethical need must be experienced by man in complete differentiation from the biological push. Such an experience presupposes two things. First, man must be a free moral personality. Freedom of action in compliance with or violation of the norm is a *sine qua non* of ethical behavior; without it, man will not experience the moral gesture as an act filled with meaning that enriches his life. Second, the unique experience of duty and responsibility is only possible if the alternative of a non-ethical act is a live option.

By contrast, take hunger, for example. The hunger-emotion was never conceived by man as a specific duty. He is driven by it and is aware of the "must" in the sense of not being able to act differently. However, there is no imperativistic component involved. The "natural must" excludes freedom, while the "ethical must" guarantees free choice.[7] Whenever I experience biological pressure, I am *eo ipso* conscious of the impossibility of resisting that drive. It never occurs to me that if hungry, I may yet refuse to carry out the demand of my organism. No choice is given, no freedom is granted; hence the experience of duty, on the one hand, and of the redeeming nature of the act itself, on the other, is lacking. A man does not feel duty-bound to do it, nor does he feel spiritually elevated when the physiological performance is completed. Only freedom secures the full ethical experience that

---

7. The postulate of freedom is necessary not only for the justification of reward and punishment, but for the legitimation of the very essence of the ethical experience. The latter presupposes the alternative of acting contrary to the ethical imperative. Otherwise, the ethical law would be reduced to the existential. In general, responsibility with its consequences – reward and punishment – is a religious (or legal) concept. The ethical experience does not imply the feeling of responsibility. Man is prompted by an ethical pressure, without an explicit awareness of the consequences of his performance.

starts with a feeling of moral responsibility and ends with the joy of fulfillment.[8]

In other words: only the alternative of sinful action introduces the specific ethical experience into the realm of human activity. If one cannot sin, his good deeds are non-ethical. Paul's objection to the law as the springwell of sin is partially correct. Yet the possibility of sin is the mother of the ethical act.

(2) Freedom is only possible if man is conscious not only of his oneness with nature, but of his otherness as well. Let me emphasize right here that man's incommensurability with nature is not based upon any metaphysical endowment in man (in the Augustinian manner), but upon a specific quality of man. There is a community of interests between man and Mother Nature so long as man considers himself in retrospect; but when he is aware of himself in prospect, there is distinctiveness and incongruity.[9] Since time immemorial, man has been wandering with Mother Nature on a common road; when he reviews himself in retrospect, he finds himself in a close embrace by her. But when man anticipates himself in prospect, he chances upon something unique – he has the peculiar ability to encounter nature and contrast himself with it in terms of I and it. There is nothing mystical about this; it is merely the cognitive drive, the cognitive gesture which requires man to face nature as something extraneous, distinct and separate. This strange capacity for splitting an absolute unity (like man-nature) is the most characteristic mark of human existence. The

---

8. It is probable that the second characteristic trait of the ethical experience, that it is meaning-giving and elevating, is a direct result of the freedom consciousness. Because I acted freely and could have violated the norm – that is why I consider my performance an accomplishment.

9. For an illustration, we may avail ourselves of a certain phenomenon in human society: the parent-child relationship. When seen in retrospect, that is, the child is the offspring of the parent, we are presented with intimacy, but when looking to the future, we generally observe incommensurability of interests, drives and motives. The modern tragedy which comes to expression in the parent-child conflict is the most conspicuous evidence for such paradoxical intimacy.

budding of freedom is at the same time the dawn of man's *noesis*, of his mental perception or intelligence, which is synonymous with encounter with nature, with the experience of otherness that is basic in him. In other words: the ethical experience must be accompanied by the noetic gesture.

(3) The breach with absolute, all-inclusive natural immediacy and intimacy and the acquisition of the capacity of encountering nature as something beyond one's reach, opposed to and different from man, is followed by focusing man's attention upon another existence, with which he enters into coexistence. While man faces nature in the role of the I (subject) facing the it (object), he approaches another subjective existence as the I facing the thou. Again we reckon with a paradoxical situation. On one hand: I and thou are two distinct existences separated by an ontic schism, which can never be bridged. The gap is by far more pronounced between I and thou than between I and it. There is complete separation and incommensurability between the I and the thou. The essence of the human personality asserts itself in absolute uniqueness and isolation. Yet on the other hand, we assume the possibility of an ontic community of interests, of fusion of motives and drives, and of a most intimate contact between subjective existences. Otherwise any social bond would be nonsensical.

But there is a major difference between the feeling of ambivalence that man experiences in encountering nature and that in meeting his fellow man. As we noted, in regard to nature, man feels one with it as long as he sees himself in retrospect, and experiences his otherness as soon as he glances at himself in prospect. In contrast, when man encounters the thou, it is the reverse: he sees separate existence when looking in review, while in prospective anticipation he begins to become aware of the intimate contact possible with the other being, of common bonds and motives.[10]

---

10. As indicated above, man separates himself from all-inclusive nature as soon as he makes an aboutface and, instead of marching with nature in a given direction, encounters nature with the first question: "What is it?" When he begins to wonder about nature, which until then was identical

Put another way, man's ties with nature are objective and real, based upon a common origin and fate; but his affiliation with another person is of an ethical-ideal type, based upon a common future and destiny. Freedom is understood only if both of these realities are appreciated: the pressure of nature's limiting necessity, and the vastness of the ethical task that demands the common effort of other individuals.

The net result of the aspects discussed above is that man as a natural being suddenly begins to discover in himself not only identity but also incommensurability with nature. Thus he enters into a new phase of viewing nature from a distance and meeting other beings who act in a similar manner. Man can simultaneously be both unique and universal; the self is both isolated, shut off in its own paradoxical existence, but also flows into the non-self, merging with others. At this phase, the personality begins to assume shape and the ethical norm attains its full meaning. Man experiences the ethical must, not as a natural necessity which he cannot flee but as a unique imperative which, if he decides so, he may disobey and ignore. By experiencing such a norm, he

---

with him, he severs the bond connecting him with his origin and appears in a new light: a subject facing an object, as an I encountering an it. The cognitive performance emancipates humanity from its bondage to nature. As a matter of fact, intelligence bent on freeing animal or man from his service to the group and on substituting his own interests for those of the latter changes his role. Until now his individual existence is irrelevant. He exists only because through him the species asserts itself. The individual constitutes the medium through which life propagation is made possible; the intelligence tells man: you exist because you exist. Your existence is self-justifying and warranting. Man delivers himself from the yoke of natural uniformity and monotony under two aspects:

(1) logico-epistemological: the theoretical gesture introduces the chasm of subject-object; he and nature forge in two opposite directions;

(2) because of the awakening of a selfish interest in his existence and placing himself in the center of the universe. Anthropocentrism is a natural attitude on the part of man. Though philosophically false, it remains psychologically true. Every person considers himself the most important being in the universe. The only question which bothers his mind is: how

contrasts himself with nature and the consciousness of freedom begins to dawn upon him.

Let us review the above-mentioned theses.

(1) In contrast to natural necessity, (e.g., hunger) which when experienced is absolute, the ethical imperative is experienced as both a must and as something that may be resisted or ignored. The realization of the ethical norm is thus enriching, redeeming and meaning-giving, whereas the natural law is only sustaining and pleasing.

(2) The ethical experience is the threshold of a personal existence. Personality does not connote anything supernatural or transcendental. It signifies only the emergence of subjectivity in man: he encounters nature and begins to face it as something alien and different, thus becoming an individual, unique reality.

(3) Two subjective, individualistic existences meet and view each other both from the aspect of full uniqueness as I and thou and of ontic merger. Freedom is possible only within the framework of a community of interests and motives. The individual within the community, isolated from and yet one with his fellow-man, is the free ethical personality.

---

can I make everything serve my selfish interests? Man as a pleasure-seeking animal singles himself out and cuts off the ties binding him with the cosmic occurrence.

As a cognitive being, he divides the world into two: the stage upon which the cosmic drama unfolds itself and the critic's box from which he observes and analyzes this performance. As a hedonic being, he places himself in the focal point and lets the cosmic occurrence spin around him. Existentially man is one with nature; culturally (noetically) he is alien to it.

In regard to other individuals (the I-thou relationship), this paradoxical experience of oneness and otherness is vice versa: existentially two personalities are completely alien to each other. Individuality denotes uniqueness and exclusiveness. I exist in a specific way that nobody else experiences. There is an unbridgeable gap separating me as an I from the thou. The feeling of oneness dawns upon me with the birth of my cultural consciousness. Ethically, I realize that there is a community of interests, a common task and destiny. Existential fate divides people, cultural destiny unites them.

In light of these premises, it is hardly possible at this point to consider the *va-yomer lahem E-lokim* as a full ethical norm. The biological drive is totally different from the ethical imperative. It is true that the biological law and the ethical imperative are identical, yet this is the *ideal* of Judaism, not its starting point. The first ethical norm cannot be reduced to the biological drive. First man must experience the specific, unique ethical norm and attain all the attributes of a personality-existence. Only then is he able to re-experience his biological reality as an ethical *telos*. The *va-yomer* remains for the time being mere information: Adam became aware of himself as a natural being. This self-awareness opened a gate to a mysterious world of personality and individuality. Man stands on the threshold of a personal existence.

Part II
The Emergence of Ethical Man

CHAPTER 5

The Emergence of Human Personality

While in the first chapter of Genesis man was not singled out and no unique position in creation was assigned to him, in the second chapter attention is focused upon man. Man seems to take center stage from the outset:

> And there was not [yet] a man to till the ground (2:5).

> And there He put the man whom He had formed (2:8).

> And the Lord God commanded man (2:16).

This chapter reviews the story of creation from the aspect of a definite anthropocentrism.

The First Ethical Norm

The second chapter begins with God characterized by the double name *Havayah E-lokim*, "Lord God." God reveals Himself on the one hand as a personality, transcendent and extraneous to the cosmos, and on the other hand as the highest principle of the natural occurrence.

> In the day that the Lord God (*Havayah E-lokim*) made the heavens and the earth (Gen. 2:4).

The account that the Torah gives of God's post-creative activity is remarkable:

> The Lord God planted a garden eastward in Eden and there
> He put the man whom He had formed (2:8).

God preoccupied Himself with developing His own creation; He cultivated a garden. This type of work is not exclusively divine. Man is also qualified to perform this task. The unique divine act of creation was completed on the sixth day, with God teaching man how to make the earth yield its fruit to him. His performance served as an illustration of how to exploit nature.

> ...and there He put the man whom He had formed (2:8).

> And the Lord God took the man and put him into the Garden
> of Eden to till it and to keep it (2:15).

Man was charged with the task of continuing the divine performance in developing the soil. He attained his technical intelligence. The propensity for technical planning, anticipating and executing was acquired by him. Still, man remained a nature-being; he looked upon himself as one with the outside world; he did not as yet isolate his existence from that of others. As a matter of fact, the whole experience of I in contradistinction with others was alien to him.

> And the Lord God commanded the man, saying, "Of every
> tree of the garden you may freely eat: but of the tree of the
> knowledge of good and evil, you shall not eat of it: for on the
> day that you eat of it you shall surely die" (2:16–17).

The first ethical norm is disclosed to man. Instead of *va-yomer,* "He said," the Torah used the verb *va-yetzav,* "He commanded." What is the difference between *va-yetzav* and *va-yomer*?

Va-yomer signifies that God informed man of a factual situation, of something which is. In our case, He told him about the biological drive. Of course, divine information implies an imperative. But man was not ready yet to experience the ethical imperative disguised as an existential law, a natural push. Such understanding is the highest achievement of man. *Va-yetzav*, on the other hand, means command. A new law in all its uniqueness was imposed upon him.[1] This law cannot be experienced in the beating of his heart, but in a new area of his existence. The new norm is completely alien to the biological impulse. The hunger appetite drives man to a certain performance without distinguishing between one fruit and another. The mere fact that among the satisfiers of biological demand one fruit was isolated and set aside as taboo indicates the unique character of the norm. Biological motivation is neutral as far as ethical standards are concerned. Man suddenly experienced the ethical imperative, which was prompted by autonomous, unique interests, unknown to natural man. He suddenly gained insight into a new force, an ethical one. With the *va-yetzav* of divine command, with the dawning of the

---

1. How ludicrous was the attack of Paul and the Gnostics upon the Hebrew Bible which concentrated upon the concept of ethical and religious law! The law, argued the Christian as well as the Gnostic, is the springwell of sin. A man would not be tempted by any object or performance if it were not forbidden to him. Had not God enjoined man from eating from the Tree of Knowledge, he would have not committed himself to a life of sin. Prima facie the argument does make sense. Adam would never have stretched out his hand toward the mysterious Tree of Knowledge if God had not distinctly pointed at the tree in a gesture of prohibition. Why did God do it? The answer is simple: the unique, ethical norm was bound to constitute itself in man's consciousness. Such a law is not urged by any biological drive. Man as a natural being is neutral to the typical moral law. Only a specific commandment could have accomplished that. The ethical norm must leave the avenue of sin open. Otherwise no freedom is granted man. Of course the law is the source of sin, but also of the singular moral act. The possibility of evading the norm – the presence of sin, gives my act the individual quality of morality. By imposing upon Adam an ethical norm, God constituted him as a moral personality.

87

ethical experience, man begins to experience his selfhood, his personalistic existence.[2]

The Evolution of Man-Personality

Immediately following the divine command prohibiting eating from the fruit of the tree, God openly observes man's social condition:

> "It is not good that man should be alone; I shall make him a help suitable for him." And out of the ground, the Lord God formed every beast of the field, and every bird of the air; and brought them to the man to see what he would call them: and whatever the man called every living creature, that was its name. And the man gave names to all the cattle, and to the birds of the air, and to every beast of the field; but for the man there was not found a help to match him (2:18–20).

Loneliness is not good for man. But what kind of loneliness was meant? Surely, not the loneliness which is synonymous with forlornness, forsakenness, the feeling of being forgotten by all with whom I have a common existential root. For such an emotion already presupposes man as a social being, as a full personality, that is capable both of contrasting its own unique existence and at the same time of sharing it with others. The lonely one who bears the full brunt of forsakenness is the most friendship-hungry person. Spiritual loneliness asserts itself in the painfulness of an isolated existence "excommunicated" from the sphere of solidarity and sympathy, in the experience of frustration and immobiliza-

---

2. I consider the three events which were related in this chapter (the injunction against eating of the Tree of Knowledge, the creation of Eve and the classifying of the animals) not as separate things whose coinciding is just arbitrary and at random, but as one occurrence. The creation of a man-personality – man experiencing ethical pressure, delineating his existence against a natural background and meeting the thou – is the same story told under three different aspects.

tion in view of monotonous distances enveloping man and his getting lost in an environment filled with dead non-personalistic beings. Such feelings signify nothing else but man's striving and longing for communion with others, his desire for an exchange of information with his fellow man. The loneliness experienced through continuously addressing oneself, in one's eternal quest for directing one's remarks to a thou, is the loneliness of the personality that is both unique and universal, isolated and sympathetic, individualistic and social.[3] Loneliness is in contrast to coexistence; monologue, to silence of the dialogue.

All this, however, has very little application to Adam in his primordial state. A non-personal being is never – can never be – lonely. It lives in perpetual solitude, but not in loneliness. The divine remark "it is not good that man should be alone" refers not to the tragedy of a lonely existence, but to a non-personalistic existence that is paradoxically both non-individualistic (completely generic) and non-sympathetic. The animal is distinguished neither by uniqueness nor by solidarity. *Levado*, "alone," in this passage denotes a state of neutrality and indifference. "It is not good that man should be alone" means: it is not good for man to remain solitary in the sense that a non-personalistic life is a life in solitude, a single life. A man-person lives in loneliness, man-animal lives in solitude.

God's intention was exactly to transform man's solitude into loneliness, his stillness into silence, his self-containment into

---

3. This kind of loneliness is not exclusively human but is divine as well. We speak of divine *bedidut*: "So the Lord alone (*badad*) did lead them, and there was no strange god with Him" (Deut. 32:12). The loneliest Being is God. He is the only one, He is infinite, eternal, all-inclusive and all-exclusive, transcendent and hiding. He is the archetype of the most unique personality and the most remote being. Creation and prophecy, His creating and addressing the thou, manifest the divine longing for communion, coexistence. The divine monologue is converted into a dialogue. Maintaining these opposites simultaneously (*coincidentia oppositarum*) is a divine attribute which the human personality emulates.

explosiveness. In other words: transform man-animal into man-personality. How did He accomplish it? By a twofold method: letting man confront nature, and the "thou."

> And out of the ground, the Lord God formed every beast of the field, and every bird of the air; and brought them to the man to see what he would call them: and whatever the man called every living creature, that was its name. And the man gave names to all the cattle, and to the birds of the air, and to every beast of the field; but for the man there was not found a help to match him (2:19–20).

Adam becomes the arbiter. Suddenly he stopped marching with nature in the same direction; he turned his face to nature (in the opposite direction) and began to wonder, to examine, to reflect and to classify. Suddenly a schism developed between man-nature and nature: the split implied in the cognitive gesture, the discrepancy involved in the subject-object division. Man is no longer a non-reflective being that forges ahead in unison with a mechanistic natural process, but begins to single himself out, to confront nature in a mood of cognitive criticism and observation. This very cognitive performance evokes the incommensurability of man and nature. Man must look upon his environment as a neutral "it," not as an opposing thou. There is no tension between the I and the "it."

Yet now that man confronts nature, he misses the community of interests and solidarity in work and purpose that he previously had with his environment. What man needs is both opposition and harmony, animosity and peace, the "against" of rebellion and the assistance of cooperation – *ezer ke-negdo*. God was looking for a thou whom man would confront face to face in a spirit of both revolt and submission. Etymologically the noun *ezer* is usually combined with the dative *lo*, "for him," not with *ke-negdo*, "against him." *Hazal* noticed this peculiarity and quoted the Palestinian saying "If he merited – she will assist him (*ezer*), if he did not merit – she will be against him (*ke-negdo*)" (*Gen. Rabbah* 17:3). A profound philosophical truth is contained in this aggadah: *ezer ke-negdo* denotes a helper who will confront him, who will challenge him; he and the *ezer* will look in opposite directions.[4] The *ezer* will be both helper and adversary, fellow-man and mysterious stranger. The I will find in the thou both fellowship and strangeness. Grammatically, the thou always faces the I into his face; the *negdo* (opposite him) denotes in Hebrew not only presence of the second person but the actual physical confrontation face to face. When I address somebody in second person, I must perform the basic movement of turning my face to him.

> And the man gave names to all the cattle, and to the birds of
> the air, and to every beast of the field; but for the man there
> was not found a help to match him (2:20).

The distinctiveness of man came to the fore; his incongruity with the animal was pronounced by the cognitive operation. A breach was completed in the immediacy of man and nature, his involvement in and oneness with the all-inclusive cosmic occurrence. Something dragged "him" out of this immediacy – and that something was his own cognitive performance. Man attained the "I" level as nature, for him, turned into an "it."

---

4. "It is unlikely that man was created to be alone in the world ... for all creatures were created male and female to bear children ... More likely, it is as the view that [humans] were created with two faces, and they were formed so that the procreative process was internal, flowing from the male organs to the female organs ... And the second face was a 'help' (*ezer*) to the first in its capacity to procreate. And the Holy One, blessed be He, saw that it is good that the 'help' stand opposite him, and that he should see it and be separated from it or joined to it at his will. That is the meaning of what He said in the verse, 'I will make him a helper opposite him'" (Nahmanides, Gen. 2:18).

The Appearance of the "Thou"

With man's secession from nature and his becoming aware of a unique normative "drive" there was need for the final step, namely, the appearance of the thou. Examining the story of the creation of Eve, we are struck by a few peculiarities.

(1) First, the biological moment of propagation and reproduction is entirely lacking. The first chapter dealt with the physiological differentiation of male and female: *zakhar u-nekevah bara otam*, "male and female He created them"; this chapter ignored it completely. Even the blessing of *peru u-revu*, "be fruitful and multiply," was not imparted to Adam and Eve in this chapter. The sexual impulse is simply not mentioned. Apparently, the primeval motif of this story is not the physiologico-biological problem but the personalistic-ethical one. God was searching not for physiological completion of the male in the form of a female, but for ethico-ontic oneness of man and woman. Adam found in Eve the personalistic thou; together, they comprised the first metaphysical community.

(2) Eve was not formed of the dust of the ground but of the rib of Adam. The moment of oneness was symbolized by that.

> And the man said: "This is now bone of my bones, and flesh of my flesh: she shall be called woman, because she was taken out of man" (2:24).

However, the language is only metaphorical: the unity here is not physical, but rather personalistic, ontic. Their oneness consisted in solidarity in work, the sympathetic understanding of a common destiny, the co-stirring of a sense of duty-morality, and comradeship in effort. Man suddenly discovered that he is lonely in his personalistic exclusiveness and individual singularity. He thus developed a dual propensity: to encounter the still, neutral, objective *it* (nature), with which ontic communication is impossible, via the medium of the monologue; and to encounter the thou who stands opposite him, who differs in essence, who exists merely by virtue of not being Adam, and be able to turn toward the other, not only with the body, but also with the soul, and address Eve. The I and the thou plunge through the dialogue into one undivided unity; the pendulum of existence swings between oneness and otherness. The mystery of the I and thou was thus revealed in the paradoxical phrase *ezer ke-negdo*. No sex-differentiation is mentioned in this chapter; the only valid separation is that of man-woman, *ish-ishah*, of two individuals.[5]

> That is why a man leaves his father and his mother, and cleaves to his wife: and they become one flesh (2:25).

Again the moment of unity is stressed. The merger is not that of mating (this is not the central theme of the story of man as a unique creature) but that of a personalistic union. The individual self loses its loneliness, the I breaks through to the thou; the I which was insanely shut up within itself has been forced to admit the thou. The fellowship of the I and the thou is the guiding motif of Eve's creation. *Ve-hayu le-basar ehad*, "and they shall be one flesh," means one personality.[6]

(3) God wanted man to emerge out of his natural solitude within an indifferent non-responsive nature into a state of loneliness-fellowship, and for this specific purpose He created another individual, in the form of a woman, a person of the opposite sex. Why? At this point we arrive at the focal problem of the story of man: to borrow a Christological term for our purposes, the Original Sin.

---

5.   Of course, the verse with respect to Noah applies the same term to animals: "Of every clean beast you shall take to you by sevens, male and female" (Gen. 7:2). Yet the expression "male and female" is of a metaphoric nature. However, in the story of Eve, the words *ish ve-ishah* retain the full primeval meaning.

6 .   Traditional commentators, such as Rashi, and some Biblical experts interpreted *ve-hayu le-basar ehad* as "out of the parents an embryo will be formed." However, this is not an exclusively human trait.

There is a controversy among theologians and Bible scholars as to the nature of the original sin. The Hellenistic theologians of the church defined the original sin as essentially lust that brought concupiscence into this world. All evil stems from sensuality.

The Paulinic-Augustinian school identified original sin with pride. Sensuality was described by that school as a consequence of and punishment for the more essential sin of self-deification. In his epistle to the Romans, Paul says that because man "worshipped and served the creature rather than the Creator, God gave them up unto vile passions." Pride leading to rebellion is the basic sin of man.

A careful examination, point by point, of the episode of man's fall (to once again borrow a Christological term) from a Jewish perspective will yield very different conclusions.

CHAPTER 6

The Tree of Knowledge and the Emergence of Sin

The Tree of Knowledge

> And the Lord God planted a garden eastward in Eden, and there He put the man whom He had formed. And out of the ground the Lord God made to grow every tree that is pleasant to the sight, and good for food; the tree of life also in the midst of the garden, and the tree of knowledge of good and evil (Gen. 2:8–9).

Of course, *be-tokh ha-gan*, "within the garden," here refers to the Tree of Knowledge as well. Eve's statement to the serpent verifies this:

> ...but of the fruit of the tree which is *in the midst of the garden*, God has said, "You shall not eat of it" (Gen. 3:3).

The central position of the Tree of Knowledge symbolizes its central role. The eating of its fruit may revolutionize man's world-formula. Let us understand that Adam's environment as depicted in this chapter was Paradise. The garden constituted man's world. The Tree of Knowledge grew in the middle. The whole garden somehow formed concentric circles around that miraculous tree.

Now, the law against eating of the Tree of Knowledge was imposed upon Adam even before Eve was created (2:17). Nevertheless, in Eve's conversation with the serpent, both of them employed the *plural* form.

> And he said to the woman, "Has God said, you shall not eat (*lo tokhlu*) of any tree of the garden?" And the woman said to the serpent, "We may eat (*nokhel*) of the fruit of the trees of the garden, but of the fruit of the tree which is in the midst of the garden, God has said, 'You shall not eat (*lo tokhlu*) of it, neither shall you touch it, lest you die'" (3:2–3).

The exchange clearly implies that both Adam and Eve were enjoined from consuming the fruit; without this assumption, God's punishment of Eve would make no sense. Apparently, the norm given to Adam was binding even in regard to the woman. The unity of the I and thou, the "and he shall cling to his wife" (*vedavak be-ishto*), asserted itself in common sense of moral duty, ethical solidarity and also in responsibility. Not only the man will die as a consequence of his sin, but so will the woman: "lest you (plural) die" (*pen temutun*). Both are partaking of the same destiny with all its ramifications; coexistence is synonymous with ethical sympathy. What had been a command to Adam became a moral dialogue, an ethical conversation between the I and the thou.[1]

---

1. The prophet as the charismatic personality who is the recipient of the divine commandment appears in a new light. How does a law addressed to the prophet bind the whole community? Many chapters in the Pentateuch are phrased in the singular form, as if Moses were the sole person accepting the law! The ontic community which sweeps away all individual bounds renders the norm all-inclusive. The prophet binds the group and passes on responsibility to its members. We will address this type of agency in the final chapter.

The Serpent's Depiction of God

While chapter 3 refers to God as "Lord God," *Havayah E-lokim*, throughout, the few sentences that report the conversation between Eve and the serpent conspicuously leave out the unique nature signified by the name of Hashem. Thus, while the opening verse of the chapter states:

> Now the serpent was more subtle than any beast of the field which *the Lord God* (*Havayah E-lokim*) had made

the very next verse, reporting the serpent's direct speech, states:

> And he said to the woman, "Has *God* (*E-lokim*) said, you shall not eat of any tree of the garden?"

The tetragrammaton (*Havayah*) was omitted. The rest of the conversation scrupulously leaves out this name of God, which is otherwise consistently employed throughout the story. Why?

The serpent's advice, vicious and evil, reflects his concept of God. God said man will die on the day that he eats of the tree's fruit. The serpent stated: God will never carry out His threat. The serpent denied either the omnipotence of God or His absolute truthfulness: "He just told you; and yet He will never carry out His threat." What the serpent actually wanted to destroy is the ethical norm. The stirring within man of a new sense of moral duty, the spiritual experience of the ethos which is enriching, deepening and redeeming of life were undermined by the serpent.

> …for God knows that on the day that you eat of it, then your eyes shall be opened, and you shall be as gods, knowing good and evil (v. 5).

The serpent depicts God as jealously guarding His prerogatives against the possibility that man might have his eyes opened and become "as God, knowing good and evil." The "egocentric" God is afraid of man, who may attain the same excellence if he were to revolt against Him. God wants to keep man in bondage in order to perpetuate His power. The serpent incites man to rebellion by challenging both divine omnipotence and divine sincerity: "In decreeing the norm," says the serpent, "God was not guided by an ethical motif; the new Law is motivated by jealousy and evil!" If God is (Heaven forbid) non-moral or amoral, there is no reason why man should be molded into a moral being. The serpent sees the God-man relationship expressed in tension, animosity and even hatred. He does not deny a personal God; what the evil, brazen serpent attempts to question is divine ethicism: God is not an ethical personality, whose will is absolute good. Hence the name *Havayah*, "Lord," the name that symbolizes God as a personality whose essence and existence are ethically good,[2] is out of place in such a portrait of God.

The conclusion is unequivocal: the serpent wanted to reduce both God and man to the status of beings endowed with highly developed mechanical intelligences – and locked in competitive struggle. The experience of God, according to the serpent, is demonic, uncanny, weird. Man should not fear God but should shudder or feel horror before Him. He created man in order to enslave him, to keep him in eternal bondage of incapacity and ineptitude. God is not the friend but the fiend, seeking only to arrest the development and progress of man. If man wants to gain freedom, he must rebel against Him and throw off His yoke. At this point, then, the cosmic tragedy of man began. The latter stumbled and fell in the net which the sly serpent spread before him.

---

2. The thirteen attributes of God (Ex. 34:6) begin with the double use of the name *Havayah*, and then proceed immediately to ethical traits: "Hashem, Hashem ("the Lord, the Lord"), mighty, merciful and gracious."

The Serpent's Personality

The immediate conclusion of such blasphemy is that the serpent, whatever sort of creature it was, appears to be endowed with personality. The latter breeds both evil and good. But even evil is a personality trait, for it is a category of morality. Not only man attained a personalistic existence but even the serpent. The ability to speak, to possess knowledge of a "demonic" God, to scheme, to anticipate a certain deed and expect consequences are all characteristics of a personality. The serpent demonstrated all those traits.

The difference between Adam and the serpent is the one which prevails between an ethical and a demonic personality. If the experience of God is fraught with all the elements of "divine demonism" (Buber, *Moses*, pp. 56 f.), then the human personality must be fiendish and satanic. The finite human personality in its primeval uniqueness is the reflection of the infinite divine. The serpent, who pictures God as a cosmic satanic ruler jealous of man and whose motives are non-ethical, is bound to become himself a monstrous demonic personality.

Personality itself is not endowed with any transcendental qualities; it emerges from the natural cosmic process. Even an animal may achieve "personality," if its technical intelligence is brought to a high degree of development. The propensity for selectiveness and discrimination which forms the inner essence of the technical intelligence hides in itself personalistic potentialities, which in turn may develop into a full-fledged unique personality. Man-animal became man-person; the serpent attained the same degree of uniqueness.

> Now the serpent was more subtle (*arum*) than any beast of the field (3:1).

In contradistinction to wisdom (*hokhmah*), *ormah* in most cases has a negative connotation, denoting slyness, cunning and scheming. It involves a technical wisdom that exhausts itself in planning and arranging attainment of practical means leading to an end.[3] The genuineness of the purpose, its ethical cogency, is of minor importance. The end is dictated by a practical-utilitarian intelligence. *Ormah* mostly implies a conspiratorial mood, disguised deceit, hypocritical behavior, malice and falsity.

Normally, a non-personal being like an animal cannot display all these negative traits. Non-morality is as personalistic as morality itself. We are forced to conclude that in some miraculous fashion, the serpent freed itself from its immediacy and identity with nature and began to feel the mysterious stirring of personal uniqueness and isolationism. However, it had not experienced the *va-yetzav Hashem E-lokim*, the divine command that produces the specific moral pressure; absent was the peculiar ethical norm with all its redeeming and enchanting power. Only Adam received that command. Thus, the serpent-personality recognized God from a cosmic-dynamic standpoint only. God appeared to the serpent as a powerful tyrant who is jealous of man and whose only interest is centered about the preservation of His privileged position. The serpent did not comprehend God as the ethical being whose power is goodness and who sympathetically shares His infinite unconditioned existence with the finite conditioned human being. Hence the serpent intoxicated himself – and man – with the infinite impossibility, that his evil imagination brought before his covetous eyes in glamorous colors. A new personality was born: the demonic, unsatiated, daring, despotic, dominating, masterful animal-persona, whether it be a captain of industry, a politician, a Don Juan or a robber baron.

Two personae thus appeared on the Biblical stage: the weird-demonic serpent-personality and the ethical-sympathetic Adam

---

3. E.g., "They acted cunningly [*be-ormah*] (Josh. 9:4); "that he acts with great cunning [*arom ya'arim*]" (I Sam. 23:22); "They take crafty counsel [*ya'arimu sod*] against your people" (Ps. 83:4); "He frustrates the devices [*mahshevot arumim*] of the crafty…He catches the wise in their own craftiness [*be-ormam*]" (Job 5:12–13).

personality. The battle lines were drawn. One persona was doomed to defeat. But which one?[4]

The Ethical and the Esthetic: The Birth of Shame

As we read through the third chapter of Genesis as it recounts the painful saga of man's fall, we notice three consequences of the primeval couple's eating of the fruit of the Tree of Knowledge: the primeval couple immediately develops a sense of sexual shame (v. 7); they fear God and hide among the trees of the Garden (v. 8); and when they are confronted by God about their hiding, they proffer a lie (vv. 9–10). We must seek to understand how violating a simple command led to such severe consequences for humanity.

Let us begin with the sin itself. In rather atypical fashion, the Torah describes Eve's encounter with the fruit in vivid, sensuous detail before she actually eats it and violates God's command.

---

4. The encounter of two personae – the demonic and the ethical – is the central theme of the fateful destiny-conscious march of Biblical Israel. The steady swinging of the historical pendulum, the mysterious curse of sin, the alternation of the ethical experience of the community, the polarity of good and evil which determined our growth, express this eternal conflict between the demonic and ethical personalities. At times it comes to the fore in the form of two individuals, and frequently the community itself incarnates both, leaping from one extreme to the other. Adam encountered the serpent, Cain confronted Abel, Noah – his generation, Abraham – Pharaoh, Isaac – Ishmael, and Jacob – Esau. Continuous strife and anguish run throughout Genesis, alternating defeat and victory. It looks as if the struggle will never end. The climax of this encounter is the wrestling of Jacob and the stranger. Who was he? Lucifer or Gabriel, demon or angel? We do not know. Yet he wanted to defeat Jacob!

Similarly, in the Sinaitic period launched in the Book of Exodus, Moses' life was dedicated to the eternal conflict. The changeability of Israel's temper and mood from nonsense to sublimity, from crudeness and coarseness to sanctity, a community first God-conscious and then suddenly idolatrous, the Israelites overcome by lust and revolting against God, and the same people surrendering themselves to God, all express the two personalities. A demonic collective meets an ethical divine personality. Both clash. It could not be otherwise. Will the struggle ever end? Yes! When? The messianic vision has the answer.

And the woman saw that the tree was good for food and that
it was pleasant to the eyes and a tree to be desired to make
one wise (3:6).

The question arises immediately: How did she see all that? Of
course she expected such results, she was enchanted by the fruit
and her imagination pictured before her mind marvelous qualities which were allegedly hidden in the fruit. The Torah depicts
here irresistible desire in the most natural colors. The latter asserts itself in a motivating force which consists of an imaginary
objective plus mental tension and continuous movement toward
the final imagined destination (see Gardner Murphy's discussion
of motivation). This irrepressible esthetic attraction is none other
than the turning point of the entire episode, the linchpin for the
Jewish understanding of man's fall, for everything that follows
flows from that physical infatuation.

Let us begin with shame, specifically, sexual shame. The Torah explicitly presents this as a primary outcome of their sin, for
right before the incident, the Torah relates how

They were both naked, the man and his wife, and were not
ashamed (2:25),

whereas after the sin had been committed,

And the eyes of them both were opened and they knew that
they were naked, and they sewed fig leaves together and made
themselves aprons (3:7).

The condition of sexual shamelessness clearly had changed; the
paradisal couple's shamelessness, their indifference to their sexu-
ality, was replaced with sexual shame, an emotion synonymous
with sensitivity, tension and passion. What does it mean?

Shame itself, as a painful self-experience, is representative of
an innate tendency in man to protect himself from scrutiny; one

refuses to allow invasion of the self by others. Infants at the age of 8 or 10 months display this trait; man's response to the curiosity of his fellow man is naturally expressed in embarrassment. It is a typical – and ambivalent – feature of personalistic existence; even as man suffers from loneliness, he tenaciously guards the most intimate secrets of his life and resents the attempt of others to pierce through his thoughts, dreams and longings.

We may distinguish two manifestations of the feeling of shame: (1) shame-experience on the aspirational level; and (2) shame-experience on the reality level (Murphy, pp. 537 f.).

Shame on the aspirational level is a common phenomenon. I aspire to attain a higher personal level, yet it is merely a hope, a dream; I am not certain that it will ever come true. I am always conscious of the schism which divides me into two: an ideal, illusory self and a real self. Shame is essentially one's feeling a dual personality, the real one and the imaginary-aspirational. Should someone suddenly penetrate my day dreams, the alter ego with whom I identify myself, and discover the ludicrous incommensurability of the two selves which I try to cover up or to forget, I experience the pain of unfulfillment more sharply. To be sure, this shame-experience of as yet unfulfilled aspirations may inspire man to new deeds and open before his eyes beckoning horizons of a beautiful world. But more often, the shame exhausts itself in a feeling of helplessness associated many a time with the deep consciousness of guilt, why I am not the self I should be.

More commonly, however, we apply the term shame on the reality-level, when the real self is incongruous with the self perceived by others. They consider him honest, sincere and reliable, yet he knows that he leads a double life: he is dishonest, false and corrupt. Dr. Jekyll is always ashamed of Mr. Hyde. A dualistic personality wants to avert the gaze from itself. In this case, shame arises when, in addition to the feeling of guilt, people are aware of a personality which is non-existent; their approval turns into serious disapproval. Of course, when the shift from approval to disapproval is sharp and strikes suddenly, the shame feeling may shatter the entire personality structure (Murphy, p. 538). In these situations, guilt and the collapse of the usual mechanism of self-defense mark the feeling of shame. The difference between aspirational shame and that of moral disapproval consists solely in the intrusion of the stranger. While in the first case the intruder discovers the better ideal self and hence by comparison disapproves of the concrete personality, in the second, he detects the corrupt one and condemns him absolutely. I resent the spying on me, the intrusion into my private affairs. It is always detrimental to my self-picture.

In either case, whether I am condemned because of an unrealized ideal or due to actual moral guilt, we see that the feeling of shame is rooted in social interrelationship. Why am I so dependent upon the judgment passed by others? Because disapproval spells doom for personal communion, it is synonymous with separateness and expulsion. Approval means sympathetic existence, ontic fusion of individual realities, coexistence. I dread excommunication by my fellow man. I am afraid of loneliness, of being suddenly shut off within the solitary cell of individual existence. Paradoxically, I enjoy my exclusiveness and aloneness because I crave for all-inclusiveness and together-existence.

Sexual shame is one of the most pronounced and decisive forms of this emotion. Through the feeling of shame vibrates the consciousness that we always experience the sexual drive in its distortion by evil. Somehow, man considers his sex-instinct as something illegitimate, sinful, and with the awakening of the drive, the sense of shame also awakens. He feels guilty of his own desires and therefore tries to hide them. Whether such an attitude is a result of social conventions and peculiar re-inhibitions, as many sex-psychologists maintain, or it is inherent in human mentality, as most theologians assert, is immaterial. The identification of the sex-impulse with the weakness and evil of the flesh is characteristic of civilized society. The I is afraid his carnal passion and sexual excitement will meet with disapproval on the part of the thou, particularly if the thou is of the opposite sex. That is why young girls blush when their love sentiments for someone, real or imaginary, are discovered. That also explains the unnatural behavior of adolescents when their sex instinct begins to awaken; burdened with a dim guilt consciousness, they are uncertain of themselves. They act as if they owed an apology for budding desires and drives. Such a unique sex experience found its most radical scientific formulation in Freudian psychoanalysis. There the libido was identified with a sinful semi-pathological desire for sex, rape and murder, for something which does not belong to me.

Let us understand the origins of moral culpability in the sex impulse. Although the latter is classified as a purely biological drive, it is clearly unique among humans; feelings of shame or lust do not accompany one's appetite for food. The very fact that religion, ethics and law all attempt to regulate the natural-organic need for sex points toward a peculiar quality which is inherent in it. For unlike food, there is an erotic nature to the sex feeling; while one may prefer one food over another, it is nonsensical to speak of love for that which satisfies the hunger-drive. When the sexual drive is converted into an erotic drive or sexual love – what the ancient Greeks called eros[5] – we begin to discern the singularity of the sexual feeling and its locus of moral sensitivity.

Two Levels of Sexual Life

We must distinguish between two different levels in sexual life: the pandemic and the erotic experiences.

The first is motivated by purely natural biological forces and is not limited to the human realm exclusively. Sexual tension and

---

5. As a matter of fact, "the Greeks distinguished between ... a heavenly and a profane Eros. ... the primal desire from whom the world is derived ... enters into the sphere of souls and in an arbitrary daimonic way carries out here ... his cosmogonic work: he is the great pollen-bearing butterfly of psychogenesis. The Pandemos ... needs only to stir his wings to let the primal fire be revealed in the body's games." Martin Buber, *Between Man and Man*, tr. by Ronald Gregor Smith (Boston: Beacon Press, 1955), p. 28.

urge is nothing but the instinctive compliance of man-animal with certain insistences of the organism. In this case, the sexual impulse is dependent on the activity of the sex-glands; that the orgiastic fulfillment of the sexual desire is accompanied by intense feelings of supreme pleasure does not alter the naturalness and organic simplicity of the performance. Animals also probably experience a similar state of excitement and satisfaction.

Most importantly, such a sexual urge does not spell a new relationship between an I and a thou. The satisfier is never conceived as a thou; it is always looked upon as an it. There is no sympathetic coexistence between two individuals of opposite sexes who are driven to each other. There is no desire for ontic community or existential solidarity; the only bond between them is the one that prevails between the I and the satisfier. There is, strictly speaking, an absence of any form of personal relationship; I am attracted to you simply because you are attractive and fascinating, physically pretty. With the discharge of the organic tension, there also expires the relationship. The I-it sexual relationship is typical of animal mating; among humans, the man who avails himself of prostitutes in moments of sexual need remains at the level of animal mating. In such cases, we cannot speak of sexual love; the genuine eros does not make its appearance while man is indulging in an animal-performance.

Erotic love, however, spells a new relationship between the man and the woman. It places the sexual desire on a new plane. Through it a new passion in man craves for self-realization, namely, the urge for sympathetic existence, for ontic solidarity and community asserts itself via a carnal-biological medium. The eternal quest of the unique, lonely individual to flee his solitude and loneliness and share his personal existence with others finds fulfillment in such a carnal merger.[6] From its loneliness and uniqueness, the I cries out through a carnal medium to the thou, begging him or her for deliverance from the misery of a solitary existence. We are all aware that wherever sexual desire is sublimated by erotic love, the lovers are lonesome for each other even when sexual desire is silent. They enjoy each other's company; they like to converse, argue, think, meditate, dream, suffer and rejoice together. The Hebrew term employed by the Bible for sexual union – *va-yeda* – also points toward cognition-recognition: the I recognizes the personal existence of the thou. The relationship changes from I-it to I-thou; the carnal community is also an existential one. Sexual objectivity and existential subjectivity blend together to bring forth erotic love.[7]

There is another important difference between the I-it experience of carnal love and the I-thou experience of erotic love. Sexual hunger of the first type makes the man or woman disregard the inner qualities of his or her respective partner. They cast upon each other the objective gaze of pragmatic appraisal; the only valid consideration is the capability of the other individual to serve as a source of pleasure and satisfaction. It is a businesslike assessment of assets and liabilities.

Erotic love-hunger, on the other hand, compels the potential lover to turn to the other human being, to the beloved, and accept her in all her otherness and independence, in her total self-reality. Friendship as such is an axiological gesture; I cannot give friendship to the thou if at the same time I disapprove of him as a personal being. The ancient Greek myth that the goddess of love is blind is false. Sympathetic coexistence is a reciprocal act

---

6.   Mystics of all the ages overburdened sexual sensuousness with excessive symbolism. The parallelism between the lustful kiss of man and woman and the beatific kiss of the souls in eternity was a commonplace in medieval mysticism. Even our prophets used sexual love as a simile for the transcendental love of God for man.

7.   The halakhic system deeply understood the metaphysical character of erotic love. All the legal details involved in the matrimonial union attest to the formation of a collective ego: *ishto ke-gufo* (a man's wife is like himself), the husband's provision of maintenance (*mezonot*) in return for her earnings (*ma'asei yadeha*), his various rights in her property (*nikhsei melog and nikhsei tzon barzel*) all attest to a personalistic surrender and concomitant acquisition of rights and privileges, to a sharing of responsibilities and duties.

of identification and valuation: each person both acknowledges the metaphysical self-sufficiency and unconditional importance of the other, and at the same time begs for acceptance and approval of oneself for redemption from the abyss of loneliness and inferiority. When a young boy proposes to a girl, when he begs for acceptance, for approval, telling her that without her, his own life will be meaningless, trivial and dull – these confessions are not the figment of a sickly fantasy, but objective descriptions of a real state of affairs. Erotic love enriches and elevates my own existence, granting it meaning, because I find my existence approved by another unique, lonely existence. Such approval is tantamount to sympathetic coexistence, to a common existence.

But we are still left with our overarching question: what actually in all this serves as the transition from the animal-physical to the erotic-spiritual, from the natural act of temporary mating to the metaphysical community of the I and the thou? How does it happen that he who himself turns to the other human being, opens himself to him, lives and faces him in the whole compression of existence, is a creature which stamps around in the frenzy of the sex instinct? Where is the miraculous bridge over which the carnal egocentric I crosses the river of sense and enters the land of an I-thou reality?

The secret is hidden in the esthetic experience itself, in pleasurable enjoyment, which is representative of the erotic life.

Pleasure as an Esthetic Experience

The prime objective of any form of biological pressure is not the pleasure experience but the discharge of tension and a flow of organic energies. The desire, as a purely organic insistence, exhausts itself in a sensation of relief and relaxation. Eating many a time just disposes of a loud demand of our body by returning it to normalcy and routine functioning; elimination of urine, while similar on a glandular level to the sex-impulse, is not a source of pleasure. The instinct is bent on relieving certain organic areas, which swell up under an excess of energies; as soon as the energies are released, the instinctive performance comes to an end.

As a matter of fact, in many cases the organically useful and spiritually pleasant do not coincide. Sometimes we are apt to think that there is malice in nature in regard to our pleasure-drive; many forms of indulgence in pleasant activities are detrimental to our physical well-being. The urge of self-preservation implanted in the organism collides with the urge of pleasure-enjoyment. But for millennia, man has been experimenting with his biological energies and tensions for the sole purpose of converting them into something for which they were not meant in the original scheme of creation: into a source of pleasure and enjoyment. Eating, drinking and particularly sexual intercourse began to serve a new goal – pleasure experience. Instead of man driven to activity by biological motivation, we find man trying to make the organism respond to external stimuli in order that he could repeat the same performance, which has become for him an inexhaustible well of *hedone*. The sexual urge, more than any other biological urge, is identical with a fervent longing for pleasure, for beauty, for enjoyment. Thus the esthetic pleasure-experience was born.

Whether beauty is "pleasure objectified" or pleasure as a quality of things, as Santayana formulated according to the contemporary theory of esthetic hedonism, is still very questionable.[8] Art incarnates something more than mere pleasure. Yet there is no doubt whatsoever that the subjective esthetic experience is that of supreme pleasure. The quality of the esthetic pleasure-experience is distinguished by three characteristic traits: (1) by its self-sufficiency; (2) by its orgiastic abundance; and (3) by its hypnotic nature.

(1) *Self-sufficiency*: Pleasure as an esthetic experience emancipates itself from the servile role of a means to an end and usurps

---

8. George Santayana, *The Sense of Beauty: Being the Outlines of Aesthetic Beauty* (New York: Charles Scribner's Sons, 1896, 1936), p. 41.

all the privileges of the latter. Instead of being a concomitant of another intentional purposeful act, it becomes the purpose, the end itself which commands the subordination of all other activities.

If we look at these independent acts of *hedone*, we see that pleasure is isolated from the complex human activity, idealized and idolized. It is anticipated before the consummation of the undertaking takes place; while everything else recedes into the background, the pleasure-impulse becomes more and more dominating. In other words, the esthetic experience is sought after, worked for and anticipated. Pleasure is being ethicized to the extent that it assumes a normative aspect. Pursuit of pleasure works itself out into an ethical "must," into an ethical goal about which all human activities are centered. Ethics is the *techne*, the "how" to achieve the complete esthetic state of mind.

When a man no longer performs an ethical deed because of the dictate of the conscience but for the sake of the performance itself (because it gives him pleasure), he is placing himself at the disposal of the esthetic impulse. Pleasure in the esthetic experience becomes self-sufficient and autonomous. The former handmaid is raised to the status of the mistress.[9]

(2) *Orgiastic abundance*: The esthetic pleasure is orgiastic; its greatness consists in the depth and extreme tension of violent, unharnessed emotions. Nietzsche was right when he said that the esthetic experience contains Dionysian elements.[10] A person is lascivious, pleasure-intoxicated, pleasure-dedicated when he gives himself up to the orgy of pleasure. There is passionate bac-

---

9. The self-sufficiency of pleasure may extend into intellectual spheres as well. When man no longer searches for truth because it is useful or redeeming but for the sake of the theoretical activity itself (e.g., *pilpul*), he is guided by an esthetic motive. He studies for the sheer delight of cognitive performance. Enjoyment as a secondary moment of the cognitive act turns into the prime objective.

10 . See *Twilight of the Idols*, ix:8–11. in *The Portable Nietzsche*, ed. and trans. by Walter Kaufmann (Viking Press, 1954), p. 518, where Nietzsche discusses the Apollonian and Dionysian elements in the esthetic experience.

chanalian surrender to pleasure and ecstasy in cultivating it. The esthetic feeling is an ecstatic experience.

(3) *Hypnotic nature*: The yearning for pleasure is a dynamic force, driving man to adventurous undertaking, to daring experiments defying danger and opposition. He intoxicates himself with infinite hedonic possibilities, which his vivid imagination brings before his mind's eye in wonderful colors. He sees in everything a pleasant recreation, a pastime, and he is never satisfied. The instinct begins to gaze at and to enjoy itself in a peculiar performance, which is determined by a hedonic objective.

Yet this type of activity is not an ethical one, although many a time philosophers have striven to identify both. It is a hypnotic activity, by which I mean that the factor of freedom is absent.[11] The pleasure-drunk person becomes an addict to the hedonic way of life. He acts involuntarily and by the sheer force of habit. Bergson said correctly when he formulated the typical esthetic hypnosis: "The object of art is to put to sleep the active or rather resistant powers of our personality, and thus to bring us into a state of perfect responsiveness, in which we realize the idea that is suggested to us and sympathize with the feeling that is expressed."[12]

Driven by the pleasure instinct, man does not actively choose between evil and good; he is not conscious of any other fear except the esthetic fear of hedonic failure. Pleasure being the common denominator of all activity, it is only the degree and intensity of the hedonic state which really matters; the rest is irrelevant. Whether to attain this agreeableness through ethical means or not is of no consequence.[13] Pleasure is an immediate datum of our experience

---

11. See Henri Bergson's discussion of "psychological determinism" in *Time and Free Will: An Essay on the Immediate Data of Consciousness*, tr. by F.L. Pogson (London: George Allen & Unwin, 1910), pp. 155 ff.
12. Ibid., p. 14.
13. Kant, in his *Critique of Practical Reason* (Abbott translation, London: Longmans, Green, 1927), made a similar point (p. 31):

    Just as to the man who wants money to spend, it is all the same whether the gold was dug out of the mountain or washed out of the sand, provided

and is basically neutral to ethical sensitivity. Its quality is hypnotic and ecstatic.

The metamorphosis of sex-pressure into an existential yearning can thus be achieved by an esthetic gesture directed upon hedonic experience. The coordinated behavior of both man and woman, striving for esthetic co-ecstasy and orgiastic co-experience, makes the consummation of this urgent desire possible. The man and woman, each seeking the esthetic pleasure-experience by use of the other, may achieve existential unity insofar as the esthetic experience implies oneness of both.

Yet this miraculous transformation of the purely physiological motivation of the sex drive into a love experience, expressing a metaphysical yearning, can be understood under an entirely different aspect: that of ethical solidarity and community of responsibilities.

Ethical Solidarity

Reading the first three chapters of Genesis, we see that the sublimation of the *zakhar u-nekevah* (male-female) relationship into that of *ish ve-ishto* (husband and wife) is a central theme of the story of man. As indicated above, the second chapter, devoted to the motif of human uniqueness and isolationism, substituted the aspect of psychological amalgamation and existential unity for that of physical mating. The verse "That is why a man leaves his father and his mother, and cleaves to his wife" (Gen. 2:24) points toward metaphysical coexistence of two singular autonomous

---

it is everywhere accepted at the same value; so the man who only cares for the enjoyment of life does not ask whether the ideas are of the understanding or of the senses, but only how much and how great pleasure they will give us for the longest time.

Arguing with the material ethic in general and the hedonistic in particular, Kant advanced the thought that if *hedone* is ethicized (declared as the ethical goal), then ethical life will become estheticized; the attainment of the goal will not discriminate between ethical and non-ethical means or qualities of the experience.

personalities instead of the role of being mutual satisfiers. However, this coalescence of two incompatible existences into one is prompted by the *ezer ke-negdo*, by the cooperative role which was assigned to both of them, by solidarity in work and responsibilities, by reciprocity of rendering services, and by the common pursuance of an identical goal. In other words, the sex impulse becomes a powerful catalyst which accelerates the realization of an existential community of two individuals with all their separateness and aloneness.

Yet it is not exclusively limited to the man-woman relationship. It may become all-inclusive, extending to a multitude of individuals engaged in a common project and bearing the hardship and suffering for an identical ideal. Love and the medium through which metaphysical merger is realized must not necessarily be reduced to a sex-love, but may rise above the organic pressure and assume a completely spiritual aspect. For the sexual motivation is not the *cause* of this union but the *means* through which it comes true.

Let us see how the original plan of creation anticipated this coalescence of *ish ve-ishto* and what precise role sexual desire played. In the first chapter of Genesis, the sex impulse is initially imparted to man strictly as biological information, implying no ethical connotation. By the second chapter, the same impulse attained a new normative status. As long as man was only conscious of his immediate, organically uniform and "unbroken" course of the life function, which has not severed itself from the primitive unity with nature, no moral aspect could have appeared on the surface. Only with the awakening of the moral agent in chapter 2 did the norm also awaken. The *va-yetzav* of divine command opened before man a new outlook, brought forth the ethical norm, which is experienced quite differently than the biological must. With the appearance of the unique ethical motif and the surrender of man to a new force, the primeval "And God blessed them, and God said to them, 'Be fruitful and multiply' " (1:28) is shifted from an organic to an ethical focus. Not only does God inform man of his biological propensities and tendencies but He commands him to follow them. The biological law works itself out into a moral law, the factum into an ideal, the to-be into a shall-be. With the revelation of the personal God, whose very essence-existence is ethically infinite and whose creative dynamics is ethical activity, the whole universal drama is converted into an ethical drama. Existence can now be termed "good": "And God saw everything that He had made, and behold it was very good" (1:31). Man's biological form of existence is not only a dull, meaningless factum, but an ethical performance.

Hence, the sexual impulse of physiological tensions and insistences now becomes fundamentally an impulse to reproduce: *peru u-revu* ("be fruitful and multiply"); it is an urge, a longing for fatherhood, a cry for maternity. In such a state of strict biological motivation, the impulse for preservation and the impulse for sexual relations constituted an indivisible oneness; they were not separate, independent functions (as they would later become under the aspect of the esthetic pleasure-experience). Nature acts ethically because God's word, the primeval *va-yomer* ("He said") of Genesis, was imbedded in dead and live matter, and God's word is an ethical word. Within the world of Genesis 1, man, merely prompted by the cosmic-natural *va-yomer* and discharging his biological energies, is *eo ipso* engaged in an ethical performance and may raise physical functions to the level of ethical realization.

Therefore, the sexual impulse might have become an ethical impulse, if only man had understood the affinity and kinship that prevails between the *va-yomer lahem E-lokim* ("God said to them") and the *va-yetzav Hashem E-lokim al ha-adam* ("the Lord God commanded man"). He would then have identified the *E-lokim* with the *Havayah* and the ethical norm with the natural tendency implanted in man. Sexual life was destined to become an ethical act. This would help man raise his sex-experience from the natural-factual to the ethical-ideal level. The erotic love of *zakhar-nekevah* would become the ethical love of *ish ve-ishto*, steeped in ethical dynamism and activation. The common basis of existence would then be a common ethical conscience, solidarity, identical sense of duty and the vision of a single purpose. The medium through which organic sex-tension turns into existential yearning would be an ethical idea.

The mere fact that the reproductive urge drives man out of his solitary, hermit-like existence into communion with another person stirs up in man a metaphysical longing for existential co-alescence. I may be conscious of the metaphysical bond existing between me and the person I love, because through my association with him or her I perpetuate in human form the communion of souls and bodies, enhanced by a mystical desire for immortality in the continuance of germ plasm and the inheritance of special qualities and faculties – *va-yomer lahem E-lokim.* If I understand this urge in its real nature, I must realize that I alone cannot perform this ethical task, for whose realization I need the cooperation and loyal participation of an equal partner. The fulfillment of my ethical duty consists in a cooperative performance, in an act realized by two individuals.

But that is not all. The divinely ordained task of man in chapter 2 (v. 15) – to till and tend the garden (*le-ovdah u-le-shomrah*) – creates a further impetus for collective life. The necessity of meeting life-emergencies and exigencies cements the unity of two. Solidarity in suffering and joy, in combating dead matter and defeating an indifferent environment, contributes to the stirring of a sense of fellowship between human beings.

Hence the ethical "must" of "be fruitful and multiply" and the imperative of survival in a callous, uncooperative setting force the I to overcome its aloofness and aloneness and join the alien thou. Both the I and the thou are inseparably united in common effort, in a primeval unity. It is existential oneness and identity, brought forth by an inter-individual ethical consciousness.

To sum up: We have seen how the intellectualization of the sex-impulse may be caused by two forces: the esthetic and the ethical. The cooperative effort of both partners who respond to each other is responsible for the sublimation of sex-pressure into an existential yearning. The coordinated behavior of both man and woman makes the consummation of this urgent desire possible. Yet this co-acting of two individuals may be apprehended as an ethical performance, the prime motif being the realization of the ontic-ethical law of the *va-yomer lahem E-lokim*, or it can be apprehended as an esthetic gesture directed upon hedonic experience. Coexistence in the first case is ethical solidarity, in the second, esthetic co-ecstasy and orgiastic co-experience. Both are subjective data, interwoven into the finest fibers of human personalism, inseparable, yet at times antagonistic and antinomic.

The Esthetic Allure of the Tree of Knowledge

Now let us return to the text in Genesis, and analyze the qualities which were inherent in the Tree of Knowledge. When we are first introduced to this unique tree, it is referred to as *etz ha-da'at tov va-ra* (Gen. 2:17).

The word tov in Hebrew has a twofold connotation:

(1) Good as an *ethical* quality – as in "I have set before you this day life and good (*tov*), and death and evil (*ra*)" (Deut. 30:15); and "you shall do that which is right and good (*ha-yashar ve-ha-tov*)" (Deut. 6:18); and

(2) good as an *esthetic* quality, meaning loveliness, pleasantness, as in "the seven *good* cows (*ha-tovot*)" (Gen. 41:26), referring to the healthy, fattened cows of Pharaoh's dream; and "a choice young man, and handsome (*bahur va-tov*), and there was not among the children of Israel a goodlier person (*ish...tov*) than he" (1 Sam. 9:2). These citations denote physical beauty. Actually, tov as an esthetic category does not signify beauty as an objective, inherent quality in the thing perceived, but rather the subjective feeling of pleasantness which the thing arouses in the perceiver. *Tov* has the connotation of the comfortable, agreeable, that which is soothing to the senses. When Eve sees that the fruit is *tov le-ma'akhal* (3:6), she means pleasant for the taste; *tovot mar'eh* would denote pleasant for the eye. "For then we had plenty of

food, and were *tovim*" (Jer. 44:17), means they were comfortable after satisfying their hunger.

Similarly, *tov*'s opposite, *ra*, possesses two meanings: the ethical sense of "evil" and the esthetic sense of "ugliness." God set before the people *et ha-tov ve-et ha-ra* – "good and evil" (Deut. 30:15), meaning an ethical choice. In contrast to the seven lovely cows, Pharaoh saw in his dream another seven cows *ra'ot to'ar*, gaunt and emaciated, meaning esthetically repulsive and unattractive.

Returning to the tree in the Garden of Eden, we must admit that the words *etz ha-da'at tov va-ra* can be interpreted as "the tree of knowledge of good and evil," as it usually is translated. Yet there is also the clear possibility of translating *tov va-ra* as beautiful and ugly. The first translation ascribes to the *etz ha-da'at* an ethical quality, while the second discovers in it an esthetic category. Let us see the description of the *etz ha-da'at* formulated in the following chapter of Genesis:

> And when the woman saw that the tree was good (*ki tov*) for food, and that it was a delight to the eyes, and a tree to be desired *le-haskil*... (3:6).

The last two properties of the tree – "that it was a delight to the eyes, and a tree to be desired *le-haskil*" – attest to the meaning of the first quality – *tov*. The Tree of Knowledge is described in purely esthetic categories: (1) *ta'avah* – the moment of lust, invincible, hypnotic desire that spells ethical atrophy and indifference; (2) *nehmad* – in the sense of attractiveness and fascination: esthetic tension brought about by the experience of beauty (*le-haskil* therefore denotes here to the eye).[14]

---

14. Onkelos ad loc. translates *le-haskil* as *le-istakla bei* ("to look at"). David Kimhi, in his *Sefer Shorashim* (Berlin ed., 1847, p. 385), s.v. *s.kh.l.* cites several other examples where *sekhel*, normally translated as "understanding," in fact means visual apprehension: "And the woman was *tovat sekhel* (1 Sam 25:3) means "beautiful to behold" (*tovat mar'eh*); "Find grace and *sekhel*

Let us take a closer look at the latter quality. *Hemdah*, the root of *nehmad*, implies an esthetic "magnetism," the quality of stirring up passionate desire and suggesting to man daring action, the power of exerting a compelling influence over and dictating certain schemes to him. The best illustration of what the Torah meant by *nehmad* is the last commandment in the Decalogue – *Lo tahmod* ("Do not covet"), which describes the greed emotion, the craving for enjoyment. Any object which brings forth such gluttonous feelings possesses the quality of *hemdah*. There is the difference between *yofi* (beauty) and *hemdah*. While the first one denotes an objective arrangement of forms, regularity and symmetry in the appearance, *hemdah* points more to the subjective responsiveness of the onlooker; *nehmad* as an adjective implies the state of being desired.[15]

While the first quality, *ta'avah la-einayim* ("delight to the eyes") denotes a purely sensuous act (seeing as a perception) stripped of all intellectual elements, *le-haskil* means seeing as an axiological performance, as an evaluating act. *Ta'avah hu la-einayim* describes Eve's immediate reaction to the tree: it aroused lust at the first glance. *Ve-nehmad ha-etz le-haskil*, on the other hand, refers to a responsiveness which is based on esthetic pragmatic appraisal of the worthiness of the object. It is worthy of being desired. Yet the worthiness of the object is measured by esthetic-hedonic standards.

---

tov" (Prov. 3:4) means "fine appearance (*mar'eh tov)*"; "Blessed is he who considers (*maskil*) the poor" – "pays attention to and looks" (cf. Kimhi's commentary on Ps. 41:2). See also Hayyim Heller, in his footnotes to the Peshita (a Syrian Aramaic translation of the Torah) on Genesis (Berlin, 1927, p. 4), citing Kimhi's translation of *nehmad le-haskil* as "beautiful to behold" (*la-mar'eh*).

15. "I believe that the tree whose name is *etrog* in Aramaic is called '*hadar*' in Hebrew, for the meaning of *etrog* is desire, as we translated *ve-nehmad le-mar'eh* (Gen. 2:9) in the sense of being desired to look upon, *lo tahmod – lo tarog* ("do not covet, do not desire"); and we say [in the *ketubah*] *mi-kol shefar arag nekhasin* – "the best and most desired goods" (Nahmanides, Lev. 23:40).

In light of this interpretation, the noun *da'at* ("knowledge") takes on a new meaning. It does not refer to *da'at* in the cognitive sense – theoretical knowing – but to the esthetic subject-object relationship, hedonic knowledge. *Etz ha-da'at tov va-ra* means "the tree of foreknowledge of the pleasant and the unpleasant" or "the tree of anticipating the agreeable and disagreeable." This is the tree of esthetic motivation, of the orgiastic tension. The term *da'at* implies more than cognitive awareness; it implies intimacy, closeness of association, sympathy with the other fellow.

> God looked upon the children of Israel, *va-yeda E-lokim* (God apprehended) (Ex. 2:25).

God saw the Israelites and He became intimate with their suffering. *Va-yeda* denotes passional knowledge, the I's sympathy with the thou.

> And the Lord said, "I have surely seen the affliction of My people who are in Egypt, and have heard their cry by reason of their taskmasters; for I know their sorrows" (Ex. 3:7).

I suffer with them in their sorrows.

Pleasure and suffering, enjoyment and discomfort are esthetic categories. Pain as a spiritual datum is an esthetic quality. *Da'at* has the connotation of an esthetic experience either in the passional or in the hedonic meaning. *Da'at* implies intimacy; hence the sexual act in Hebrew uses the term *da'at*, for it is typical of the orgiastic co-experience of both partners. "And the man knew his wife Eve" (Gen. 4:1) should be translated "And Adam became intimate with his wife Eve"; both co-experienced the same desire and its fulfillment.[16]

---

16. Even the term *da'at et Hashem* may be translated "intimacy with God," enjoyment of the divine glory. Maimonidean intellectualization of *da'at Hashem* is not necessarily true.

As a rule, *yada* and *da'at* apply not only to theoretical knowledge but also to awareness through the senses as well.

Which removes the mountains and they are not aware of (Job 9:5).

I have not been aware of myself, my soul set me amongst the chariots of a princely people (Song 6:12).

... and acquainted with sickness (Isa. 53:3), implying suffering with disease.[17]

We thus reach the conclusion that the tree awakened lust, was pleasant to the eye and fascinating in its appearance. Hence *etz ha-da'at tov va-ra* corresponds to the esthetic quality of the beautiful and the ugly. God forbade man the orgiastic esthetic experience, the acquisition of the pleasure-impulse; he was not allowed to overemphasize the moment of wantonness, making the beauty ideal the fascinating force in human life.

The Sin of Pleasure as Its Own End

Man ate of the tree and experienced pleasure, not as a secondary phenomenon, a concomitant to something else, but as an end in and of itself. Eve ate of the tree for a single reason: the tree was beautiful. Eve became fascinated, enchanted by the miraculous fruit; all her faculties of resistance melted and the omnipotent drive of lust overwhelmed and made her sin. Adam and Eve turned into hedonic beings; pleasure as a motif became central in their lives. Sex-love therefore became an addiction to *hedone*, surrendering to the violent, orgiastic reckless experience, lived through all human passions, feeling their full range and highest tension. The sex urge was sublimated into an esthetic urge; the yearning for coexistence through a carnal medium found fulfill-

---

17. See Radak ad loc.

ment in hedonic co-experience of hard sensuous pleasure and emotional compulsion. The ethical aspect was eclipsed entirely.

Surveying the development of man after the original sin incident, we notice that the Torah places special stress upon fascination by beauty. As we analyzed above,[18] the general background against which we must observe sin is *hamas*, violence. The act of overreaching myself and reaching out after something that does not belong to me, invasion of existential areas that are beyond my sphere of existence, constitutes the springwell of sin.

> And it came to pass when man began to multiply on the face of the earth, and daughters were born unto them, that the *benei ha-elohim* saw the daughters of man that they were fair; and they took them for wives of all which they chose (Gen. 6:1–2).

Man began to multiply, and the division of existential areas came into being, a reality that *eo ipso* should have led humanity to feel the full pressure of the ethical duty to respect alien property and rights. Yet some men, the *benei ha-elohim*, saw the women that they were fair and were attracted by their loveliness. In consequence, they reached out after the forbidden lovely and fascinating women, and grabbed them. The ethical motif collided with the orgiastic esthetic one and was defeated. The passion in man aroused by beauty was too powerful. He yielded to a new force in life – dynamic, hypnotic and compelling – and stepped over the boundary line of his individual sphere of existence. Whenever the Torah warns Israel against sin it uses the simile of esthetic fascination: *Lo tahmod* – "you shall not covet," i.e., be fascinated by *hemdah* – by pleasure which is magnificent (Ex. 20:14); "that seek not after your own heart and your own eyes after which you used to go astray" (Num. 15:39).

The term *zenut*, which the Torah applies to all kinds of sin

---

18. Part I, chap. 2, p. 33.

in general and to sexual and idolatrous indulgence (the orgias-
tic-bacchic cult) in particular, refers to the irresistible, esthetic
sweep to which man surrenders; he is swayed by a motif which is
ecstatic, bacchic and orgiastic, powerful and ruthless, the motif
of pleasure frenzy. This unsatiated hunger and unfulfilled desire
for the unlimited *hedone*, the continuous movement toward the
pleasant and agreeable, is *zenut*.

> ...but you have played the harlot (*zanit*) with many lovers
> (Jer. 3:1).

> Yea, you have played the harlot with them (*tiznim*), yet you
> could not be satisfied (Ezek. 16:28).

> ...their straying (*zoneh*) heart...and their eyes which go
> astray (*ha-zonot*) after their idols (Ezek. 6:9).

The lustful glance, which is adultery in itself, the lack of loyalty (an
ethical category), betrayal, change of affects, the steady quest for
new sources of pleasure, the ingenuity in discovering or inventing
artificial stimuli and unwarranted desires – all these qualities constitute the excessive hedonic experience. Sensuality unhallowed
by ethical appraisal is *zenut*.

To be sure, *zenut* as such conveys lasciviousness. Yet *zenut*
in the sense of idolatrous worship implies another element – that
of religified wantonness, the orgy, the bacchic frenzy, as a divine
cult, as a service, as the only medium through which man may
contact the gods. The Dionysian cult is the esthetic, reckless, lewd
worship of an orgiastic god who himself is a pleasure addict. The
Torah was ruthless in combating this notion of the pagan world.
We may say that at this point Judaism revolutionized the human
scale of values. Instead of serving God through the esthetic-ec-
static experience, the Torah commands man to worship Him via
ethical dynamism. There is no redemption for man in the esthetic
experience. On the contrary, quite often it drives him to depravity

and lewdness. There is, however, salvation in the ethical gesture. While the pagan world tried to estheticize the ethical, Judaism is bent on ethicizing the esthetic. Whoever knows a little of the ecstatic worship teeming with wild dances, thrilling music, extravagant rites which would take place on the festivals dedicated to Adonis, Osiris, Dionysus and other pagan gods can appreciate what the Torah understood by *zenut*.

It is typical of the original sin that the moment of seduction was introduced into the story of the Tree of Knowledge. Man did not sin because he chose to violate the divine injunction. Adam was seduced by Eve, and she in turn was seduced by the serpent. The human tragedy did not originate by free choice but by a hypnotic force – the esthetic experience with all its compelling power. The first sin was perpetrated in a mood of esthetic revolt which was not fomented by a free man but suggested to him by the serpent. How ludicrous the apology of Adam and Eve sounds:

> The woman whom You did give to be with me, she gave me of the tree, and I did eat (3:12).

> The serpent seduced me, and I did eat (3:13).

The defense spelled indictment; the excuse, accusation. The sin asserted itself precisely in the word *hishi'ani* – "it has seduced me": "the serpent has exerted a hypnotic influence over me, awakening the orgiastic, hedonic motif in me which deprives me of my ability to freely exercise my ethical power of judgment." Man was swayed by the serpent; the human ethical personality was captivated by the demonic personality.

Man and demon confronted each other; they collided, and the demon won the battle. Faust and Mephistopheles met. Who is the demonic personality? The serpent. What are its basic qualities? The esthetic drive which asserts itself in parasitism. Coexistence expresses itself strictly in the common enjoyment, in hedonic passivity and non-creativity. No longer do I desire the woman and love her because with her and through her I shall realize my ethical creative aspirations. My longing for coexistence is completely dominated by my pleasure-frenzy, which is self-centered, self-warranted and utterly exclusive. Instead of sharing existence with the other one on the basis of parity – the I and the thou equally form a coalition of existences – I unite with the other individual on autocratic premises – the I enslaves the thou. Power is an esthetic category. In the eternal quest for dominion man is guided by a hedonic criterion. Lust for power is lust for pleasure. The yearning for a metaphysical union becomes distorted by an evil esthetic quality – merger through absorption of the other one.

Domination as Part of the Esthetic Experience

Enjoyment is synonymous with power. I enjoy it and *eo ipso* I dominate, enslave it. The hedonist looks upon the whole world as an object consecrated to a single purpose: to be enjoyed by him. He becomes egocentric, self-loving and self-adoring. He reaches such proportions that the real object of his wantonness is not so much the sensuous pleasure he derives from the item as the knowledge that this object was dedicated to the comfort and joy of the "selfish self." In other words, the esthetic experience consists of two elements: pleasure-sensation and the exercise of domination over the satisfier. This type of dominion is distinguished by its ruthlessness and insatiability. No barriers are strong enough to stop the aggressive pleasure-conscious demonic personality from its daring aggressive undertaking.[19] It does not recognize any other existential area except its own, and it enjoys its liberation from all restrictions. This liberation is never identical with ethical freedom; on the contrary, it represents liberation from the ethical pressure of the norm, which means surrender to the hypnotic pressure of the esthetic "must."

The serpent is both pleasure-starved and dominion-hungry.

---

19. The phenomenon of jealousy, from which curse modern man has not freed himself, is indicative of the political factor involved in the esthetic love-experience. I am jealous of the other man not because he limits in

The mere fact that he made an effort to seduce Eve indicates his desire for power, for influencing others and mastering their destiny. He exults in others' dependence upon his advice and finds pleasure in ruling them. The esthetic personality is the masterful, dominating personality. *E-lokim* for the serpent is representative of an estheticist-God who created the world in order to enjoy it afterwards, a God who enjoys His creation by enslaving and dominating it. The dynamic God is both powerful and orgiastic. He wants human beings for the sole purpose of keeping them in bondage and rejoicing in their ignorance and stupidity. The pleasure-loving God is fearful of the competition of man, who may find out how to master his own existence. God exercises a vast technical intelligence; whatever He created is destined to satisfy His desire for power. Therefore, man, for the sake of his own good, should revolt. The whole controversy which raged in antiquity and the Middle Ages about the nature of the original sin – whether it consisted in the discovery of sensuality or in the act of revolting against God – may be satisfactorily resolved. The esthetic experience, as indicated above, is both a pleasure awareness and a domination exercise.

The orgiastic enjoyment is rebellious, anti-authoritarian. The demonic personality wants to play, it matters not with what; it wants to find outlet in something, it matters not via what medium. It rejects authority, it frowns upon all injunctions. The esthetic appetite is stimulated by a boundless fantasy. Fantasy lets an enchanting, beautiful mirage arise before a hungry, passionate glance wandering in yellowish desert sands and weaves a myth of pleasure for a starved soul. The main motif of *hedone* is *hemdah*, desire for something which has not yet been reached and which is beyond the boundary line of legitimate realization. *Hemdah* drives man to drink the dregs of the cup of pleasure and wring them out. This limitless passion is revolt. If God is powerful and

---

any way my hedonic possibilities and opportunities but for his usurping rights and privileges pertaining to my wife. Not the lover but the master feels humiliated by treacherous, illicit love.

enjoying His existence endlessly, then man attempts to compete with Him, to interfere with His designs which man deems detrimental to his esthetic self-realization. It is peculiar that when Genesis describes the antediluvian deterioration of man in terms of *hamas*, it uses the term *elohim*.

> And it came to pass when man began to multiply on the face of the earth... that the *benei ha-elohim* saw the daughters of man that they were fair; and they took them for wives of all which they chose (Gen. 6:1–2).

The *benei ha-elohim* encountered the *benot ha-adam* ("daughters of man"). Who were the *benei ha-elohim*? The sons of the privileged few, of the masters, of the robber barons who thought that they were entitled to everything and that no law was applicable to them; men who practiced *hamas* for the sake of enjoying life.[20] If the woman is fair, attractive and stimulates desire, then why not take her prisoner and exploit her for purposes of wantonness and lewdness? *Mi-kol asher baharu* – "all which they chose." The esthetic choice guided by esthetic stimulus and sensuous response determined their actions. *Benei ha-elohim* were typical of the

---

20 . Many of the medieval commentators explicitly find some form of hamas in these verses:

> "That they were fair (*tovot*)": Rav Yudan said: it is spelled *t.v.t.* (and can be vocalized *tavat*, implying improving something), [meaning]: when they improved her appearance, beautifying her to enter the marriage canopy, the ruler would enter and have relations with her first (Rashi).

> "*Benei ha-elohim*" – 'The sons of princes and rulers' – this is Rashi's view, and so it is in *Bereishit Rabbah*. If so, Scripture relates that the judges whose duty it was to administer justice among them openly commit violence (*hamas*) and no one stopped them... when the daughters of men were fair, they would coercively take them as wives for themselves. And Scripture tells of the violence (*hamas*) and mentions further, "whomsoever they chose," in order to include those women who were married to others (Nahmanides).

demonic personality, of the God-concept which the serpent formulated: a powerful, egocentric and ego-enjoying God. On one hand there were fair women who stimulated desire, invincible sex-gluttony, and on the other hand the *benei ha-elohim* who ruthlessly reached out after the beautiful women.

Conclusion

It is natural, then, that the immediate change precipitated by the eating of the forbidden fruit expressed itself in the feeling of sexual shame. Adam and Eve began to feel embarrassed in exposing their genital organs. Why? Because the sex-urge was now distorted by the pleasure desire. Each of the partners began to feel the pressure of guilt and culpability. Eve became the desired lovely person with whom Adam wanted to merge his existence for the sheer delight of possessing her. Sympathetic intimacy is here determined by a sinister longing for dominion and exploitation, for demoting the other individual to the status of a slave.

Had the sexual love represented ethical solidarity and co-responsibility, the guilt moment would not have appeared at all. Partners would in such a case crave for each other in an ethical mood; equality and reciprocity would be the foundation of the existential union realized through carnal means. Yet man freed himself from the fetters of the ethos, and yielded to the esthetic hypnosis. The straightforwardness and simplicity of the urge disappeared; it became carnal and complicated. The partners

---

It is likely [that Scripture means] they took women forcibly. (Ibn Ezra).

"*Ve-ahot Tuval Kayin Na'amah*" ("the sister of Tubal-Cain was Na'amah") – However, our Rabbis have another midrash concerning her which states that she was the extremely beautiful woman on account of whom the *benei ha-elohim* erred, and she is the one hinted at in the verse, "and the *benei ha-elohim* saw the daughters of men" (Nahmanides 4:22).

As the midrash connects them, the beautiful woman who kindled the passion of the *benei ha-elohim* was called Na'amah – "loveliness."

must stimulate each other, kindle one another's fantasy; the bond lost its permanency and turned into a transient, one-time urge for coexistence. The coexistence is indeed subordination of each other, and the longing for it is amoral. The pleasure and comfort of the partner is irrelevant. My interests come first. Man began to hide his desire, for it spelled the humiliation of his partner. He acquired the feeling of shame.

CHAPTER 7

Further Consequences of the Sin: Fear, Lying and Punishment

As we continue through the third chapter of Genesis, we observe two further consequences of man's first sin: (1) fear; and (2) the lie.

Fear

For the first time man became aware that he is afraid of God and fled from before Him.

> And they heard the voice of the Lord God walking in the garden in the breeze of the day: and the man and his wife hid themselves from the presence of the Lord God amongst the trees of the garden.... And he said, "I heard Your voice in the garden, and I was afraid, because I was naked, and I hid myself" (Gen. 3:8, 10).

Why did man and woman fear God? Because they began to compete with Him.

Instead of love implied in the ethical performance of emulation, tension developed between man and God. If man, impressed by the demonic description, is conscious of God who is non-ethical and who seeks to dominate His creation for the sake of sheer pleasure, then he must experience in the proximity of God horror and shuddering, uncanniness and strangeness. Divine friendship became infinite animosity; divine wisdom, cunning; love, jealousy. Affirmation of existence by God turned to negation. God is exclusive and unique in the sense that He desires human existential plight and misery. All the characteristic traits of the religious experience like awe, the feeling of daunting, *mysterium tremendum*, are typical of the demonic personality who retreats, flees, and hides before God.

A new chapter was written in the God-man relationship. God pursues man, frightens him. Man seeks refuge and haven from the trailing shadow of infinity. Suddenly, the cry of a hunted animal fleeing a fiend is heard in the jungle of existence. Man has never regained complete peace with God. The "I was afraid... and I hid myself" became the curse of humanity. The greatest personalities could not free themselves from that sinister feeling of tremor and terror. God claims the entirety of the human being, and this claim displays the basic features of "tyranny" and "ruthlessness." *Ve-nakeh lo yenakeh* – "who will by no means clear the guilty" (Ex. 34:7). Why? Not because God is not fair. It is only because man tried to become a tyrant.

Biblical examples abound with this motif. God conquers the one to whom He addressed Himself:

(1) It is told that Hanoch (Enoch), who "walked with God," was taken away by Him (see Martin Buber, "Divine Demonism," *Moses* [1946], pp. 56–59): "And Enoch walked with God, and he was not, for God took him" (Gen. 5:24). Why? For Enoch apparently tripped and did not deserve divine friendship.

(2) God gave a son to His chosen one, Abraham – and demanded him back. God is called *pahad Yitzhak* (Gen. 31:53) – "the horror of Isaac" – for the latter's destiny was interwoven with that of divine "animosity" at the *Akedah* (Binding of Isaac). Why did God act this way? Because many a time Abraham erred and forfeited his privileged position.

(3) When Moses encounters the divine revelation in the burning bush, he hides his face because he is afraid to look at

God. He is haunted by fear. When God sends Moses to Egypt to discharge a historic task, on the way to that land He appears as a nocturnal visitor and wants to kill Moses. "And it came to pass on the way, in the place where they spent the night, that the Lord met him, and sought to kill him" (Ex. 4:24). Why? Moses probably appeared to be unworthy of his mission.

(4) The Jews at the Sinai revelation stepped back and refused to witness the greatest of all miracles.

(5) Jeremiah in his Lamentations exclaims out of despair and forlornness:

> The Lord was as an enemy, He has swallowed up Israel, He has swallowed up all her palaces, He has destroyed his strongholds (Lam. 2:5).

> He was unto me as a bear lying in wait, and as a lion in secret places (3:10).

The psalmist complains:

> Where can I go from You, and whither can I flee from Your spirit? (Ps. 139:7).

The flight of man from God is the flight of the demonic personality who converted love into antagonism, fellowship into tension. Jewish ethics as promulgated by the prophets undertook to heal the breach which developed between God and man. Moses' greatness expresses itself in his combating the divine terror, in his eternal longing for, and being fascinated by, God. God wanted ethical fellowship, solidarity; man chose tension and enmity. God let man carry the burden of divine antagonism. Our prayers and hopes are centered around the eschatological vision of cosmic peace between man and God.

That the God-man relationship implies intimacy as well as separateness and otherness, love as well as tension, proximity as well as infinite remoteness, rejoicing as well as mortal fear, is a truism in Jewish philosophy and Halakhah. The mere word *kadosh* has the connotation of a separate, wholly other existence. Before the Sinaitic revelation God enjoined the people from coming too close to the mountain:

> ... whoever touches the mountain shall surely be put to death (Ex. 19:12).

The priest is not allowed to enter the sanctuary simply any time he wishes:

> that he come not at all times into the holy place within the veil (Lev. 16:2).

The reason is clearly formulated in the continuation of the verse:

> for I appear in the cloud upon the ark cover.

God is present there. Sometimes divine presence spells doom for the finite creature:

> For this great fire will consume us (Deut. 5:22).

> Do not come near (Ex. 3:5).

The halakhic injunction against uttering God's personal name, the Tetragrammaton, outside of the Temple boundaries attests to the *pahad* moment, the fear which is inherent in the halakhic consciousness.[1] The pronouncement of God's name spells the appearance of God.

---

1. *Sifrei Naso* 39.

In all places where I cause my name to be pronounced (*azkir*),
I will come to you, and I will bless you (Ex. 20:21).[2]

Hence man should never try to contact God in such an intimate fashion, as he would be overwhelmed by the awe-ful, terror-inducing divine presence. Intimacy with God was recommended but not always encouraged. God is an ambivalent force.

Even the grammatical persona in our reference to God is changeable. We begin our blessings in the second person, with "thou" (*atah*), and end with in the third person, with the he form of the verb (e.g., "who sanctified us"). There is continuous alternation between the esoteric (*nistar*) and the exoteric (*nigleh*), between the hidden and present God.

Even our prayer contains this paradoxical idea. It includes both approach and retreat, confidence and dread, love and estrangement at the same time. The three opening blessings of the *Amidah* – the quintessential prayer performance – convey the paradoxical nature of the God-man relationship. The first two, *Avot* and *Gevurot*, embody our faith in a *Deus revelatus*, a God who addresses Himself to His creation, either through the perennial Israel-history (beginning with Abraham) or the dynamic cosmos (healing the sick, resurrecting the dead). He is adored as the God of our fathers and as the master of the universe. The third blessing – "You are holy and Your Name is holy" – embodies the cry of the finite being who suddenly realizes that, notwithstanding the closeness of the Creator to His creation, the distance between God and man is endless. Only our eschatology foresees the full reconciliation of God and man. The Lord will, at the end of time, appear to man, not to desert him any more.

---

2. As noted in some midrashim, *azkir* (lit. "I pronounce") can be exchanged with *tazkir* ("you will pronounce").

Lying as a Human Institution

Man was not only afraid of the divine, fleeing from Him, as a result of the sin. Associated with the original sin is also the lie.

> I heard Your voice in the garden, and I was afraid, because I was naked; and I hid myself (Gen. 3:10).

This was perhaps the most gruesome feature of the paradisaic tragedy. He set the precedent of lying, and the lie was established, I would say, as a human institution. It led the psalmist to brand all men "liars":

> I said in my haste (alarm) all men are liars (Ps. 116:11).

Why did Adam lie? What compelled him to speak hypocritically to the Lord? The answer is simple. The feeling of guilt awakened in him a sense of embarrassment coupled with fear. Man fled God because he was aware of his culpability and did not dare to encounter his Creator. The first lie is the defensive lie. The sinner was seeking to deceive his conscience. Man rebelliously attempted to break away from himself by misrepresenting himself, by lying to himself. Man suddenly became aware of a tragic conflict, which developed in his personal existence with the surrender of man to the orgiastic experience.

What was the nature of that sinister breach in the human personality? Existential consciousness was split into conscience and esthetic self-consciousness. As it was intended in the primeval scheme of creation, man appeared as a harmonious being, not torn by inner strife; his consciousness was his conscience as well. His theoretical consciousness, which expressed itself in *cogito ergo sum* ("I think, therefore I am"), was at the same time an ethical conscience, asserting itself in the awareness of the ethical need and necessity. The same consciousness which said to man "you exist" also told him "you exist as a moral being." For the *va-yomer* and the *va-yetzav* – the biological law imbedded in dead and live matter on the one hand, and the moral norm implanted in the mysterious recesses of the human personality on the other – were inseparably merged. Existence itself was experienced both ontologically and ethically.

However, with the tragic event of the original sin and identification of the ontic experience with the esthetic-hedonic surrender, a schism has arisen in human personality. The existential will now expresses itself in the perennial esthetic hunger and parasitic enjoyment – to exist means to enjoy existence in an orgiastic manner, to get the most out of it, to dominate it as the object of my lust – whereas the ethical will expresses itself through a new moral agent called "conscience." Both assert themselves in theoretical and practical judgment. The esthetic egocentric self-consciousness says: "I exist, and existence itself is synonymous with pleasure. Hence I must indulge in pleasure." The ethical conscience repeats the same formula on a different plane. "I exist, and existence itself is an ethical experience. Violation of the norm spells non-existence."

When the conscience makes its presence felt on certain occasions of wrongdoing, it protests against the esthetic ego, the self-centered consciousness that, motivated by the overwhelming craving for pleasure, throws down all normative barriers which block the road to orgiastic indulgence. The sinful esthetic personality, therefore, invented the lie as a defense-mechanism against the onslaught of the ethical personality. The defensive lie is a lie born out of panic and confusion; it is the echo of the cry of a torn personality, or rather of a dual personality: ethical and demonic.

At this point Judaism demonstrated its optimism in regard to human nature. Here lies one of the basic differences between Jewish and Christian theologians. The latter consider man to be completely depraved and corrupt because of the original sin: man created in the image of God turned into a man-Lucifer, he fell from the spiritual to the carnal plane, and only a supernatural act of salvation may save him from his misery and plight. Judaism, by contrast, maintains that man just acquired a different set of standards or split his primeval harmonious ego into two conflicting personalities. His ego may express itself through a dual medium; he may act under two contradictory aspects. Whenever he sins, only a part of his personality is involved. Only the demonic, orgiastic personality enjoys the corrupt deed; the ethical one rebels against it. Otherwise, the voice of the conscience would never be heard. The inner core of human personality remains pure and aloof. Exactly for that reason Jewish thinkers never considered the outcry of the conscience as the voice of God the way Christian theologians used to. The latter were compelled to adopt such an argument for the sole reason that they could not comprehend who else could reprimand the sinner; surely not the sinner himself! All the agony and suffering usually associated with a guilty conscience could not come from the corrupt and accused personality itself. The authoritarian character is certainly transcendental.

Judaism disagrees thoroughly with this view, however fascinating it may be. God speaks not through the mysterious conscience. It is not the angry God who meets men via the conscience; man meets himself there.

The idea of repentance is based upon this realization. Only a part of the personality was contaminated by sin; the full, original self has not been affected. The sense of shame which is associated with a guilty conscience embodies, as we noted above in chapter 5, the dual personality represented by an accused sinner and a strong, just and prosecuting arbiter. Yet both the sinner and the prosecutor-judge speak through our divided, multiple self. There is no divine interference with our most personal affairs, sin and wrongdoing. It remains a human function, which brings forth the duality in personalism. The voice of the conscience is an act of self-accusation. However, there is no division into animal and angel, body and spirit, as it is usually conceived. Here, two personalities confront each other: one equates the ontic-experience and the passional, hedonic experience; the other one brings his existence to a forceful expression in a living, activated ethos. One is orgiastic, the other the normative personality. *Teshuvah* (repentance)

136

implies rebirth of a harmonious personality by returning to God and *eo ipso* to one's own selfhood.[3]

The cry of the conscience is the cry of the true, primordial selfhood which was falsely misrepresented by a pseudo-demonic personality. Conscience is the miraculous mirror in which man sees himself in the light of an ethical existence. It is self-knowledge acquired the hard way, through pain, anguish and sorrow of the heart, caused by a sudden realization that whatever was done stems from an alien stranger that wrenched us away from our genuine

---

3.   Maimonides (*Mishneh Torah, Hilkhot Gerushin* 2:20) exploited this philo-sophical idea for the elucidation of a halakhic principle: *kofin oto ad she-yomar rotzeh ani* – "he is coerced until he says 'I want to.'" The right of *beit din*, the Jewish court, to enforce the ethical code is based upon the assumption that the true personality is always good.

> When the law requires that he is forced to divorce his wife, and he does not want to divorce [her], the Jewish court in all places and at all times beats him until he says "I want to [divorce her]," and he writes the bill of divorce and it is valid.... And why is this sort of divorce not invalid, for it is coerced? Because the term "coerced" is reserved for someone who is pressured and compelled to do something that he is not Biblically obligated to do, such as someone who is beaten until he sells something, or gives it as a gift. But someone whose evil inclination overcame him to violate a commandment and commit a transgression, and he is beaten until he does that which he is obligated to do, or until he distances himself from that which he is forbidden to do, this is not considered "coerced." To the contrary, he "coerced" himself through his wicked thought. Therefore, a person who does not want to grant a divorce, since he wants to be part of the community of Israel, and he wants to perform all the commandments and distance himself from the transgressions, and his inclination overcame him, once he is beaten until his inclination submits and he says "I wish [to give the divorce]" this is already considered willful divorce.

Maimonides speaks of an act of violence which is perpetrated by the *yetzer* ("the evil inclination") against the true original self, which always wants to act in unison with the moral law. Sin is always committed under duress. The self is intimidated and forced to act in violation of the ethical norm. The state is duty-bound to help restore man's real identity and deliver him from the fetters of esthetic bondage.

free self. The suffering of a sinner comes with the awakening of man from a somnambulistic mirage of being somebody else.

In order to protect himself against such an embarrassing experience, man avails himself of the defensive lie. "I have not done it! I have always been good!" The lie is born out of the dialogue between the conscience and the self-centered pseudo-self; it is the apologetic answer given to the prosecuting personality. The conscience asserts itself in conversing with an alien personality, with which man identified himself.

The lie would have been an impossibility had man not sinned. Why? Let us inquire into the nature of this novel phenomenon.

Types of Truth-telling and Lying

Truth and falsity constitute a central halakhic theme. The laws of *edut* (testimony, evidence), *ne'emanut* (trustworthiness), *shevu'ot* (oaths) and *nedarim* (vows) deal with the problem of truth-telling and lying. However, we must distinguish between two classes of lies.

The "historical" or "theoretical" lie consists in the form of logical judgment about an alleged fact which proves to be non-existent. In other words, any logical predication which does not correspond to an objective existence is a lie. (Let us define falsity in a most primitive manner.) Truth, as Aristotle defines it, "photographs" reality; falsity has no parallel in the objective order. When I say "This is gold," and in fact it is iron, I lied. I predicated of something which does not exist. The same applies to the historical lie, when the predication is formed in the past tense. In other words, man's speech, unfolded in logical judgments and grammatical sentences, must conform to an objective order.

Truth and falsity are not only theoretical qualities but ethical ones. When the scientist is searching for the hidden truth, he is guided by both a cognitive and an ethical motive. There is an ethical norm interwoven within the cognitive fabric of our consciousness. To make a false statement means to err not only theoretically but also ethically.

However, we must further distinguish two classes of proposition, which contain both predication and prediction: the scientific and the ethical. The scientific prediction is, in fact, an assertion of a present state of affairs that must ultimately lead to specific results. It is always a proposition related to a certain causal complex, of which the causes are given and the effect necessarily anticipated. In other words, it centers around an existing datum. For instance, when the meteorologist states "There will be rain tomorrow," he does not predict the future but predicates of the present: the atmospheric conditions prevailing at present must produce rain some time soon. His utterance consists of a twofold act: (a) description of the extant causes; and (b) explanation of the forthcoming effect via the medium of causalistic necessity. His judgment must be considered either a theoretical truth or a falsity.

The ethical prediction, on the other hand, cannot be classified as a logical proposition, because it predicates of an ethical imperative instead of a fact about reality. It does not describe a real datum but an "imaginary" ideal duty. Its domain is never "that which is" but "that which shall be"; hence its grammatical structure is the imperative rather than the indicative. When I say "I shall help my friend," I do not refer to any causal data which will necessarily produce an effect in the form of a good deed in the future. It is unique because of its free normative character. I shall help my friend, although I am not compelled to do so and I have the alternative to act differently. The ethical prediction cannot be equated with the logical predication, for it does not assert anything real of an object. If my promise does not come true, it renders my prediction not "false," but a "lie," because in the ethical realm, "truth" means not photography of reality (as it does in the theoretical realm), but creation and constitution. In a corresponding way, in this realm "falsity" means vanity and futility. The theoretical truth is descriptive and explanatory; the practical, creative.

The immorality of the lie is therefore twofold: the theoretical lie about the real environment is immoral because it distorts facts, for it does not understand the existing natural order, and God apparently wanted man to be an objective spectator of the cosmic drama. The practical lie is immoral because man's decision, if not realized, is a vain futile act not bearing any fruit, and man must be creative. That is why the terms *shav* (vain) and *sheker* (falsity), used in the two versions of the Decalogue (Ex. 20:7 and Deut. 5:11), are synonymous: an oath that is false is also vain and useless. Upon this consideration rests the whole legal structure of contractual agreements. The crux of any legal obligation is the validity and binding capacity of the human promise. The oath and vow with all their implications manifest the almost metaphysical quality of the commitment.

Truth, according to our viewpoint, is thus a twofold category: genuine understanding of the objective order, and real creativity within it. Falsity expresses itself either in the incommensurability of judgment and fact or in the vanity of the promise. The logos is not only a means of communication but an instrument of creative activity. As such, it must never be used in vain.

God, the source of creation, is true in the sense that He is the truth itself.[4] He is truthful because His thought is identical with reality; also His will is real in the sense that His mere willing is a creative act. Thus, there is in the expression "and God said" (*va-yomer E-lokim*) a triple identity: thought, will and deed. Man should emulate God and speak both the factual and ethical truth. The data about nature must be apprehended in accordance with their objective order; the promise must be translated into existence.

Man's sin consisted in betraying nature by establishing himself as a privileged being entitled to the unique right of enjoying existence without contributing to its survival. In the original intention of creation, man was supposed to remain natural – that is, coordinated with the universal existential process, forming one primeval whole with his environment. God only wanted man to

---

4. When Jeremiah says (10:10) *Va-Hashem E-lokim emet*, he means not "the God of truth" but "God truth."

be self-conscious of his individuality and uniqueness insofar as he conceives his existence as an ethical performance. Man encounters nature and *eo ipso* he abandons his non-reflective, instinctive union with his environment and substitutes instead an intelligent, free, ethical, cooperative effort. He severs his primordial bond with Mother Nature in order to tighten his intimacy with and closeness to her. Naturalness is moral, unnaturalness is sin. As long as there is mutual utility and thorough cooperation and exchange between man and nature, the lie is unthinkable. Nature lies not, nor should the natural man.

However, man betrayed his environment by giving his allegiance to a new ideal, which is unnatural – *hedone*. Man singled himself out not as a natural being who does not possess anything else beyond the capacities and capabilities inherent in him, as a biological being, but as a superior creature that is bent on conquering its environment and exploiting it. Thus man duplicated his selfhood by introducing a parasitic, esthetic personality, and this double self asserts itself in a double mode of living. This duplicity and duality brought about the lie, both the theoretical and the practical: the first one as the apologetic defensive lie, the second one as the vain promise.

Punishment

Biblical retribution is based upon the concept of *kishalon ha-het*, the failure of sin. Sin itself spells failure. The futility of sin is a commonplace in Judaism. The sinful act forfeits its own objective. No success can be attained through a non-ethical performance. This maxim derives its validity from the equation of existence and ethos. Whatever is beyond the boundary of the latter is non-existent. Hence the whole problem of the relationship between the means and the end is futile. An ethical end can never hallow the non-ethical means, since such a means would never produce the desired result.

Hence, the original sin which consisted in introducing the esthetic, orgiastic moment into man's life must lead to failure and disappointment in this very undertaking. Man was intended to co-operate with nature, and he betrayed the trust put in him and be-came a parasitic being craving pleasure and dominion. Therefore his hunger for power and enjoyment must never be satisfied.

This incessant pursuit of an ever-fugitive satisfaction, the full and yet poignant restlessness of a creature who seeks happiness and to whom even peace is denied, is the natural outgrowth of the original sin.

> I will greatly multiply your sorrow and your conception, in sorrow you shall bring forth children and your desire shall be your husband and he shall rule over you (Gen. 3:16).

We may break down this pronouncement into three separate ele-ments: (1) procreation associated with pain and sorrow; (2) never-satisfied desire; (3) instead of Eve dominating her husband (as the objective of her craving), he will dominate her. Let us inquire into the latter two.

Epicurus famously remarked, "Give me cheese and barley meal, and I will compete with Zeus for happiness."[5] However, he is in fact not happy with so little. Why? Because the curse of sin trails him. The orgiastic craving does not liberate the woman from subordination. On the contrary, it enslaves her more and more. The eternal tragedy of the woman who feels lonely and forlorn in her solitary single state, who craves a companion and yet pays the price, is implied in the divine curse imposed on her. If the erotic pleasure moment of the sex-experience was isolated from the whole and idolized as such, then the main function of the sexual union – reproduction – would be turned into a source of pain and sorrow. Nature avenges the treachery of the woman by letting her attain just the opposite result. Instead of the hedonic experience

---

5. *Vatican Sayings*, #33; see also Diogenes Laertius, 10:11; Aelian, *Varia His-toria* 4:13.

she expected to obtain from a biological insistence, she was subjected to a passional experience, full of pain and suffering.

Adam was burdened with a similar curse:

> ...cursed is the ground for your sake; in sorrow shall you eat of it all the days of your life; thorns and thistles shall it bring forth to you; and you shall eat the herb of the field; in the sweat of your face shall you eat bread, till you return to the ground; for out of it you were taken (Gen. 3:18–19).

The penalty imposed on Adam is parallel in its essence to that of Eve. Tension between fallen man and nature, and the failure of man to obtain his objective, form the main moments of the curse. Instead of cooperation, nature will display malice and hostility toward man. Betrayal of his environment by man is encountered with enmity and resistance. Man will never be capable of attaining satisfaction. Everything pleases, nothing contents. Man will restlessly wander from object to object, drain one pleasure to the dregs to try the next, feel all the weariness of satiety with each as it passes and anticipate a new source of pleasure. All this manifests itself as characteristic of the esthetic experience. Yet pleasure is many a time just sorrow and suffering; the *hedone*, pain and passion.

As a pleasure-seeking creature, man becomes unnatural and nature resents this apostasy, which is a source of continual disappointment.

As a matter of fact, even the serpent, the diabolic, esthetic personality, was condemned to eternal boredom and dullness. "Upon your belly shall you go, and dust shall you eat all the days of your life" (Gen. 3:14) implies the absence of joy and pleasure. The demonic self is penalized by his eternal dissatisfaction with life.

Conclusion

In recapitulating this section of the book, we may arrive at the following conclusions:

(1) Man was created as a natural being and was intended to

remain attached to his environment. Personality emerges from the hidden recesses of a nature-existence. *Tzelem E-lokim*, the divine image, was implanted in man as a part of the cosmic occurrence. Yet personality may evolve in two opposite directions: the demonic-orgiastic and the ethical. The ethical personality abandons its immediacy only so far as it becomes a reflective self who encounters nature in a cognitive-ethical mood. The ethical man considers himself part of the natural entirety and is guided by identical designs and motives. However, the esthetic personality confronts Mother Nature in a pragmatic hedonistic mood. Precisely this utilitarian aspect is unnatural.

(2) The ethical personality is not transcendental. It only reconsiders its own status in a normative light, conceiving the natural law as identical with the moral law. Man encounters nature, separates himself from his environment in order to merge with it again. Yet his subsequent merger is an ethical free performance. The esthetic personality severs its original, primeval affiliation with nature for the sole purpose of dominating it. It never reconciles with its parent-nature. Enmity and mutual dislike prevails between man and environment.

(3) The paradoxical tragedy did not consist in a metaphysical metamorphosis. It duplicated human personality by adding a new pseudo-self, who many a time speaks and acts on behalf of the true original whole ego. Sin did not corrupt man but split him. The task of Judaism is not salvation of a depraved existence but liberation of the real genuine I from the bondage to a pseudo I.

In the most dramatic manner, the Bible depicts the deterioration of man, who was driven at enormous speed to the abyss. We analyzed the *hamas*-concept. Man became selfish, treacherous and unnatural. God condemned man. Creation of man seemed to be an absolute "failure," *kivyakhol* (as it were).

And the Lord repented that He had made man (Gen. 6:6).

God regretted the creation of man. The orgiastic, esthetic type dominated mankind; *hamas* was the guiding motif of human activities and the demonic superseded the divine personality. The catastrophe by which God punished man – the deluge – did not solve the problem completely.[6] It improved man; yet it did not heal the breach in his personality.

Through devious ways and zigzag channels providence began to realize a new human personality: the charismatic. Abraham was born, chosen and charged with a mission by God. Abraham was selected to rehabilitate man and to reinstate him to the ideal position which he was destined to occupy. *Kivyakhol*, God needed charismatic man to appear on the human stage.

---

6. God confirmed again the fact of evil involved in human existence:

> ...and the Lord said in His heart: "I will not again curse the ground any more for man's sake; for the impulse of man's heart is evil from his youth; neither will I again smite any more everything living, as I have done" (Gen. 8:21).

He only reconciled with this state of affairs and absolved nature of its co-responsibility for man's crimes.

Part III
The Charismatic Personality

CHAPTER 8

The Charismatic Personality: Abraham

The rift in the human personality we have seen unfold over the first three chapters of Genesis, the deviation from the united ideal of creation engendered by the primeval couple's pursuit of *hedone*, called for a unique type of person who would restore the unity of the ethical and the esthetic. The process of the realization of the charismatic personality is described in the biographies of the three patriarchs and Moses. Let us begin by analyzing the figure of Abraham, the first Jew.

The Loneliness of Charismatic Man

The closeness of man and God is confined to a specific environment in spite of both divine universality and ubiquity and the effort of man to transcend his limitedness and finitude. The encounter of God and man is conditioned by certain external factors. The first appearance of God to Abraham, as recorded in the Bible, was associated with the command of *lekh lekha*, "go forth from your land" (Gen. 12:1), of emigrating from his father's home to the Land of Israel. Abraham, acting under God's orders, arrived in Canaan. God's promise to and agreement with Abraham were subject to the fulfillment of the above-mentioned command.

Why God could not enter into an intimate relationship with Abraham in Mesopotamia and had to guide him into a new land is an old problem. Judah Halevi, in his *Kuzari*, explains it with the uniqueness of the Land of Israel as an ideal land for the meeting of

God by man.[1] He attributes metaphysical qualities to the land and endows it with a spiritual climate: *hayyei neshamot avir artzekh* ("the air of your land is the breath of life for our souls" – Judah Halevi, *Tziyon, ha-lo tish'ali, Tish'ah Be-Av kinot*). Of course, the old myth of the temperate climate which is ideal for the development of man was exploited by Halevi. Nahmanides, in his commentary to Lev. 18:25, followed in Halevi's footsteps, as did the mystics. For them, the attribute of *kedushah*, holiness, ascribed to the Land of Israel is an objective metaphysical quality inherent in the land.

With all my respect for the *Rishonim*, I must disagree with such an opinion. I do not believe that it is halakhically cogent. *Kedushah*, under a halakhic aspect, is man-made; more accurately, it is a historical category. A soil is sanctified by historical deeds performed by a sacred people, never by any primordial superiority. The halakhic term *kedushat ha-aretz*, the sanctity of the land, denotes the consequence of a human act, either conquest (heroic deeds) or the mere presence of the people in that land (intimacy of man and nature). *Kedushah* is identical with man's association with Mother Earth. Nothing should be attributed a priori to dead matter. Objective *kedushah* smacks of fetishism.

I believe, rather, that the divine commandment to Abraham to leave his parents' land and go to the Land of Canaan should be understood under a different aspect entirely. The charismatic personality must disassociate himself from his national connections and completely free himself from the environment he was born and reared in. The chosen person severs his affiliation with his clan and friends; he deserts everybody in order to give himself up to his new friend, God. The first prerequisite for prophecy is loneliness. A lonely man finds the Lonely God, and this very loneliness creates the charismatic bond between them. The charismatic person must lose his country and home, he becomes a miserable stranger and straying wanderer: *arami oved avi* – "a

---

1. *Sefer Kuzari*, II:9–14; 22–24.

straying Syrian was my father" (Deut. 26:5). The commandment of God in reference to Abraham's journey emphasizes more the spiritual detachment from his childhood environment, the need for complete alienation of his heart from his kin.

> Go out of your country, and from your kindred, and from your father's house, to the land that I will show you (Gen. 12:1).

The *spiritual* straying away is the gist of the command; the physical journey is of secondary importance. Abraham must forsake his past and transplant himself into a new historical dimension. Otherwise he cannot become the favorite of his God. He is a lonely soul, an uprooted personality. His synonym is *ivri*, wanderer or a "yonderman" who came from beyond the river, a man who does not belong here. He was told to leave an urbanized society which enjoyed a highly technical civilization (technical magic) within almost a corporate state and move on toward a primitive land, where nomadic and semi-nomadic tribes wander to and fro in the wilderness with their flocks of sheep and goats and pitch their tents in many places, yet stake roots in none. We know from many reliable archaeological sources that such nomadic civilizations clashed many a time with the urbanized civilizations of Mesopotamia and Egypt. In the Babylonian kingdom in the last quarter of the third millennium BCE, the "Wall of the West" was erected as protection against the nomad Amorites. In Egypt, the state erected the "Wall of the Ruler" at the beginning of the second millennium BCE in order not to permit the foreign hordes to come down to Egypt (Buber, *Moses*, p. 26). The house-dweller hated and despised the nomad, the rover, the tent-dweller. Apparently, God preferred the latter and chose the shepherd as his confidant. Moreover, He selected a member of a stable society and converted him into a nomad. Severance of all ties with an urban, closed environment was the *conditio sine qua non* for the realization of the covenant.

Why is the charismatic person forced to be the loneliest, most detached person from society and driven from its nest?

(1) God does not share His beloved person with society. The charismatic person is dedicated solely to God who brings about events. That is why God tolerates no intrusion by society upon His befriended Abraham. He is jealous of his consorting with others. The human being acting under divine orders is portrayed as a forsaken person whose only friend is God.

(2) God Himself appears here under two different aspects: as master and owner of the entire being, as *Hashem E-lokim* who rules the world from above, to whose absolute will and authority man must surrender; and as friend, comrade and confederate who wanders with His chosen person. God takes His friend along and leads him into the wilderness. The motif of the Song of Songs prevails throughout the narrative of the lives of the patriarchs.

> Come, my beloved, let us go forth into the field; let us lodge in the villages. Let us get up early to the vineyards (Song 7:12–13).

The girl wants to lead her beloved away from the city life, from the peering eyes of the crowds and multitudes, into the solitude of the field, into the quiet, still lodgings of the villages. Love asserts itself in the desire of both partners for privacy and isolation. Spying curiosity of the stranger desecrates the holiness of intimacy. Love, exposed to public view, becomes vulgar and coarse. The self-sufficiency of both lovers expresses itself in their flight from the crowd. God and Abraham seek to escape the big cities of Mesopotamia into the pastures of Canaan.

(3) In the straying of Abraham from his father's house ("when God caused me to wander from my father's house" [Gen. 20:13]), the motif of freedom and revolt comes to the fore. The charismatic person is anarchic, freedom-loving and anti-authoritarian. Let us not forget that both Egypt and Mesopotamia developed a highly centralized state. The king and the ruling caste exercised absolute power over the lives of the subjects, who were kept in a state of semi-serfdom. Egyptian society was a pyramid society,

which culminated in its apex with the king. All customs were bound up with the strictly regulated rites conducted daily by the king. It was very important to preserve the customs unaltered. A collective slave economy supervised by taskmasters with whips, a very conservative, almost stagnant code of mores, manners and ethics, an unbearable political tyranny, religious despotism and an all-pervading state authority remind us of the modern totalitarian society. The regularity of Nile inundations was reflected in a symmetric, disciplined society. Within the framework of such an organized state, the covenant between Abraham and God could not have materialized. The first condition for this is the casting off by man of all the responsibilities and duties which were imposed upon him by human authorities. Bondage to man excludes divine friendship. The beloved must tear down all the social and political barriers that fence in the individual and imprison his initiative and liberty. The charismatic person is anarchic, liberty-loving; he frees himself from all the fixed formulas and rhythms of an urbanized civilization and joins a fluid, careless, roving nomad society. An ancient Egyptian document describes the nomads as follows: "Here is the miserable stranger.... He does not dwell in the same spot; his feet are always wandering. From times of Horus he battles, he does not conquer, and is not conquered" (Buber, *Moses*, p. 25). The stranger is indomitable; he may lose a battle, yet he has never lost a war. He will never reconcile with political subjection. Roaming, wandering, he will escape persecution and oppression. When the need arises, the nomad stands up and fights for his freedom and many a time proves superior in battle to the settled king. Abraham's heroism on the battlefield is the best illustration.

The "Anarchism" of Charismatic Man

Yet it is important to distinguish between the anarchic tendencies of the charismatic person and those of the orgiastic, esthetic type. While the moral law is completely alien to the latter, it is the guiding motif for the former. The Epicurean aesthete displays utter disregard for any kind of norm or regulation. There is a total suspension of any imperative life, negation of the supremacy of an ethos. The Biblical anarchy does not assert itself in the negation of the norm as such but in non-compliance with man-made law. The charismatic person revolts against a non-moral legalistic society, whose ends and objectives often collide with the basic tenets of a natural, living morality. He refuses to obey an external authority and to accept the dicta of a society that is guided by a highly technical, though magical, civilization. He prefers spontaneity to artificiality, improvisation to the routine. The moral law is revealed to him by his God, who is at once friend, comrade and master, and who speaks from beyond and within his own personality. The source of the law is the *mahazeh*, the prophetic vision, not the royal decree. The charismatic person discovers the ethos himself. As a free personality, he goes out to meet the moral law with his full collected being; he chances to find it in himself and to consciously adopt it. He is not overpowered by an unforeseen element. There is a free act on his part in dedicating himself to a universal, natural morality. His sovereign freedom has not been restricted. Only later does he find out, to his surprise, that with the moral law in himself he has discovered the God of morality beyond himself, and at a still later date he becomes acquainted with this unique being. God encroaches not upon his personal freedom; on the contrary, God helps him to develop his moral spontaneity and creativity. He just wants him to be His friend, to walk before and with Him – "walk before Me, and be perfect" (Gen. 17:1) – and be perfect in accordance with his own moral law.

There is no imposition of divine authority upon the charismatic person. Only a bilateral covenant, which binds both man and God, was concluded.

> And I will make My covenant between Me and you, and will multiply you exceedingly (Gen. 17:2).

God addresses Himself to Abraham not in the commanding, authoritative tone of the Lord but in the comradely, friendly manner of a fellow wanderer. He wants a covenant with him. God, as it were, is lonesome and He is anxious to find a companion. Fellowship between God and man is the motto of Abraham's life. The divine imperative was presented to Abraham as an entreaty, or rather as counsel. It was always tied in with the great promise and vision, as if to say "The fulfillment of My norm, Abraham, will perpetuate our comradeship and make you great."

> Go out of your country, and from your kindred... and I will make of you a great nation, and I will bless you, and make your name great (12:1–2).

> ...and you shall be a father of many nations... and I will make you exceedingly fruitful, and I will make nations of you, and kings shall come out of you... you shall keep my covenant therefore, you, and your seed after you in their generation.... Every man-child among you shall be circumcised (17:4–10).

In many respects God was closer to Abraham than He was to Moses. An intangible feeling of tenderness lingers over the relationship of God to Abraham. There is the creative ardor, moving devotion and a lack of tension. All that God requests of Abraham is destined to promote the latter's happiness and greatness.

Even in the *akedah* episode, the absolute imperative is lacking. God entreated Abraham; He implored him to give away his only son. He never commanded. He just uttered a wish, and Abraham complied. The absolute command entailed in *hukkat olam* ("eternal statute") is non-existent in God's contact with Abraham. True, the latter conceives the divine request as a norm: *asher amar lo ha-E-lokim* – "as God had told him" (Gen. 22:3). Yet God abstains from commanding.

> ... because you have done this thing, and have not withheld your son, your only son (22:16).

The tone is almost solicitous.[2]

The charismatic personality is a political and social anarchist who negates the authority of conventional institutions and man-made mores; he is not an ethical conformist who just subjects himself to an external authority, which overpowers and enslaves him. His God did not pursue him and take him prisoner. He did not appear to him suddenly through a fear-inspiring vision nor did He encounter him with an absolute imperative that leaves no choice but surrender. He did not demand absolute obedience and subordination. All He solicited for was loyalty, devotion and

---

2. Prima facie, the *akedah* is truly an exception to the comradely relationship between God and Abraham. There Abraham faces not a fellow-wanderer, a confederate who shares human woes and joys, but an omnipotent, jealous master to whom man is enslaved and who almost ruthlessly lays claim to the entirety of human existence. The strict legalistic relationship between lord and tenant comes to the surface. There is a demand on the part of the master for absolute surrender of the servant. God takes complete posses-sion of His friend to whom He addressed Himself. The breach between God and man has apparently not been healed; there is still tension and conflict. Divine terror supersedes divine grace and love. Confederate turns into foe, "lover" into "pursuer." The Bible never tried to eliminate the tremor mo-ment which was introduced by Adam. It just wanted to reconcile it with the covenant idea. At certain times the covenant expressing fellowship is thrust aside and God appears as the powerful master, who withdraws from the community and who denies to man companionship and sympathy. The God of the sacrifice reveals Himself, and man has no alternative but to surrender. Yet how did Abraham take this divine command? Did he argue, plead, beg for mercy and clemency? Did he ask God the dreadful question: "If I am to sacrifice my son, what is to become of the great promise?"

We marvel at Abraham's sedateness, complacency and peace of mind. The enormous feat of the knight of faith was demonstrated not in his actual com-pliance with the divine order but in the manner in which he behaved in the face of the most puzzling divine absurdity. The blood-chilling fear of meet-ing the nonsensical did not overcome Abraham. Abraham's performance is not to be equated with a compulsory submission to a tyrannical power who overwhelmed him; nor should it be understood as an act of fatalistic despair, resignation to a fate which he cannot alter and which encounters man with animosity and malice. Abraham's deed was not born out of de-spair and anguish. Far from it. Abraham did not realize the absurdity and the paradoxality of the divine order, which canceled all previous promises

friendship. He let Abraham find the ethical law, or "God's way to do justice and judgment" (Gen. 18:18). The nomad discerned his own non-imperativistic, fluid ethical code. Later God approved of these standards. The charismatic person is a daring, adventurous personality who, driven by wanderlust, explores parts unknown and horizons which beckon to him from endless distances. His adventure culminates in finding a new land and a new God.

The God-Man Covenant

The charismatic personality is fully dedicated to his God; yet God is not only a master but a friend, a fellow shepherd as well:

---

and covenants. He was not cognizant that by requesting Isaac, God actually annulled everything, including the fellowship between Him and Abraham. Naively, almost irrationally, did he conceive the demand as somehow compatible with the whole. He carried it out as if it were another means leading to the realization of the eternal covenant. Abraham was great in his acting in accordance with the logic of the absurd. By acting the way he did, Abraham unconsciously relieved the tension and reconciled himself with God.

The *akedah* became indeed the motto of the covenant and its symbol. An absurd cruelty was transformed into a great, heroic deed, which changed the historical situation of the entire covenant community at a single stroke with a basic stirring of all the elements in the charismatic personality. All creative forces of the covenant were set to work. The latter was deepened and became all-inclusive. From then on, the covenant spelled mutual, inherent, all-inclusive belonging. Man sacrificed himself to God, and God dedicated Himself to man. Earlier promises and events were recast in a new light. Instead of the primitive covenant which embodied a mere utilitarian agreement like any other treaty negotiated between two individuals, a new covenant came into being, a covenant of an existential community of God and man. The awe-inspiring moment was converted into an eternal passion. The reconciliation between man and God expressed itself in the unique covenant experience even at the moment of absurdity and nonsensical despair, in overcoming the conflict between promise and reality. Faith represents this peculiar attitude of leading a life fraught with realities which contradict the very ideal for which the faithful suffer. The charismatic person is steeped in the covenant, believes in it notwithstanding all crises and retreats. When God stopped Abraham from his sacrificial performance, He employed an almost solicitous tone. For the first time, we meet with the moment of *yir'ah* (dread, awe): "that you fear God" (Gen. 22:12). The covenant was strengthened and took on a new meaning.

The Lord is my shepherd, I shall not want (Ps. 23:1).

...the God who has been my shepherd all my life long (Gen. 48:15).

Divine authority is not regal or extraneous but immanent and comradely. God is a member of the pastoral fellowship, or of the nomad society. His imperative is valid because man agreed to such an arrangement. It is a contractual obligation, designated for the preservation of a social relationship. The covenant bridges the metaphysical gap separating man from God. The latter casts aside all transcendental traits. It introduces the invisible master into the nomad order. The formation of any social group is described by the Bible as the conclusion of a covenant, with mutual rights and obligations. Of course, Abraham is dedicated solely to God. Yet human devotion is reciprocated by God with identical loyalty. The ideal of the charismatic personality is not theocracy, but a covenant society.

The covenant (*berit*) motif is a perennial aspect in Jewish history. God is a bridegroom, a friend *and* a king – yet a freely elected monarch. He wields the authority of the elder of the clan who was entrusted with the task of guiding the pastoral group. There is always a bilateral agreement between God and man. God came to man after the latter had sought and found Him. Only then did He contact Abraham. God never derived His authority from the cosmic aspect, or from His omnipotence, but from a historical factum: covenant, redemption.

"I am the Lord your God, who has brought you out of the land of Egypt" (Ex. 20:2).

Jewish morality is covenant morality, observed by both God and man. Both form an ethical community. Instead of *imitatio Dei*, we may call it ethical solidarity and cooperation with God.

Our concept of freedom includes two different aspects: (1)

the possibility of not conforming with the norm; (2) the free acceptance of God as both master and comrade who participates in the realization of the ethical norm.

From this point, it is the concept of covenant that is to be the central theme in our considerations.

Jewish moral law is covenant-law, freely legislated between the lonely, straying, charismatic person and an invisible, unique, lonely God, who joins the band of wanderers. Hence Jewish history is covenant history. Examining the different types of covenants described in the Bible, we will find that all of them constituted turning points in Jewish history. Each covenant represents a historical level upon which certain events unfold and specific motives assert themselves. Jewish history expresses the fellowship of God and man. Halevi and Nahmanides of old emphasized time and again the unique character of the Jewish historical occurrence by placing it directly under divine protection and vigilance. The historico-coincidental forces are superseded by transcendental-purposive motives. While the universal historical process is completely dominated by the *E-lokim* aspect – uniformity and regularity, similar to the monotony in the cosmic drama, are characteristics of the historical occurrence – the charismatic historical emergence is guided by the *Havayah* idea.

The uniqueness of Jewish historical development was already formulated in Exodus:

> You have seen what I did to Egypt, and how I bore you on eagles' wings and brought you to Myself. Now therefore, if you will obey My voice indeed, and keep My covenant, than you shall be My own treasure (*segulah*) from among peoples: for all the earth is Mine (19:4–5).

Segulah means "a possession which is withdrawn from the general family property because one individual has a special relation to it" (Buber, *Moses*, p. 105). Israel occupies a singular position among all nations. Its peculiar development takes place under unique circumstances and influences. It has direct contact with God: "and brought you to Myself." The peculiarity consists not in a specific relationship of God, as master and ruler of the world, to a charismatic group, but rather in His entering and associating Himself with a chosen people. The idea of "chosenness" (*behirah*) conveys special divine association instead of domination. Israel is God's people on the basis of social realism. Covenant history connotes the involvement of God in the historical occurrence. Not only does God direct the destiny of His people, but He also entangles Himself in their historical fate and marches along with them. Israel is dedicated to *Havayah* not only as its lord but also as its comrade and co-participant in the covenant society. Man is dedicated to God and vice versa. God is loyal to man. The history of the covenant is the story of God-man friendship.

Such a fellowship between God and His people is the central motif of the Biblical narrative, seen especially with regard to the patriarchs in the book of Genesis:

Sojourn in this land, and I will be with you (26:3).

And, behold, the Lord stood above it (28:13).

And, behold, I am with you, and will keep you in all places to which you go, and will bring you back to this land; for I will not leave you, until I have done that which I have spoken to you of (28:15).

I am God, the God of your father, fear not to go down to Egypt (46:3).

I will go down with you into Egypt, and I will also surely bring you up again (46:4).

God wanders with Abraham, with Jacob first to and from Syria and later to Egypt, and leaves the land of Pharaoh together with the children of Jacob. He stops with Israel at each station and continues the wanderings with them throughout the forty years.

> At the commandment of the Lord the children journeyed, and at the commandment of the Lord they encamped: as long as the cloud abode above the tabernacle they remained encamped (Num. 9:18).

This symbol of divine presence in Israel and His involvement in the destiny and participation in their sorrows and joys was conveyed by the Tabernacle, the *mishkan*:

> Let them make Me a sanctuary, that I may dwell among them (Ex. 25:8).

As long as the Jews were nomads, roving and wandering from place to place and pitching their tent everywhere, building houses nowhere, God's sanctuary was just a tent – the *ohel mo'ed*. When the Jews gave up their nomadic civilization and became a settled, agricultural people, the divine tent was converted into a house – *Beit Hashem*:

> For I have not dwelt in any house since the time that I brought up the children of Israel out of Egypt, even to this day, but I have walked in a tent and in a tabernacle (II Sam. 7:6).

Later in midrashic and still later in mystical writings, the concept of *shekhinta be-galuta*, "the exile of the Divine Presence," developed. However, the idea of divine implication in the historical occurrence is as old as Jewish history itself.

CHAPTER 9

Charismatic Man as a Historical Personality

At this point we may take up a new problem. The charismatic person as a member of theo-society, bound by a covenant, is at the same time a historical personality. Covenant expresses historicity, emergence; hence the member of the covenant is endowed with historico-creative qualities.

The Paradox in the Experience of Historical Consciousness

Among all aspects of the historical occurrence one is most outstanding, namely, that of the time paradox. History swings between two conflicting poles: change and constancy. On one hand, history is synonymous with a continuous flow of events, characters and situations. Historical phases and periods supersede each other; the old relinquishes its place to the new, which was born in order to become old and transmit its message to its successor. A stagnant culture loses its historical prerogatives. Heraclitus' maxim, "Being is a steady flux of phenomena," may easily be applied to historical reality. On the other hand, history is marked by persistence and consistency. Parmenides' maxim that "Being is absolute identity" is as valid as the Heraclitan maxim of change. Historical events display both continuity and identity. In spite of the historical diversities, there is historical uniformity of the occurrence in general. Otherwise, it would be ridiculous to speak of morphology and certain universal patterns and determinants in history.

This dichotomy, which prevails in the historical drama, is the crux of the philosophical problem in history, and is rooted in the historical time consciousness. History, as a human event, unfolds itself in time. Yet, the experience of it is interwoven with a unique paradox. On one hand, time experience asserts itself in the fleeting, vanishing change of events. Each infinitesimal portion of time is experienced as something transient, undurable, passing, which can never be recaptured or retained. It is conceived as an arrangement of temporal instances on a scale of "before" and "after" that are not interchangeable. Events run from an irreversible past into an anticipated future. Past means the grammatical "it was," which has ceased to exist; future means the designation "not yet." History is distance in time in both directions. We look in retrospect and become aware of the remoteness of events enveloped by the nebulae of canceled existences. We glance in prospect toward a dim future and marvel at the distance separating us from non-realized existences.

Yet there is an experience of closeness in historical time. Instead of being a straight line extending in two opposite directions, time presents itself as a three-dimensional magnitude – past, present and future – that envelops the historical consciousness, that explores not only the traces of a bygone past retained in memory and a non-existent future anticipated in fantasy, but a living past and future which are projected against the backdrop of the present. The historical texture is woven of past and future; it is a focus in which the bygone and the expected converge. To live historically means to live through *all* the phases of history, both past and future. Historical pride in bygone achievements, apprehension of, and anxiety for, anticipated national disasters expresses this particular interest. The historical personality takes in the "non-existent," or, more accurately, the "not-yet-existent."

A historical community extends into both the past and the

future. Its membership includes the living, the dead, and the not-yet-born. Historical awareness is multi-temporal. If this is true of universal history, then it is all the more true of Jewish history. There is no doubt that we are very close to historical events which took place in a remote past. Our experience of the Egyptian exodus and of the giving of the Law reintroduces us into the dawn of our history with such emotional intensity that it is hardly possible to describe it psychologically. The Bible for us is not merely a book of antiquity, a historical record of deeds that led to the establishment of our nation, but contains for us a living, moving drama, which is performed by ourselves and by our ancestors as well. The Jew is not conscious of historical remoteness or temporal distance. The past is for him by far more real and concrete than for any other people.

Our two-thousand-year-long attachment to a desolate land in the Middle East, the future of which we had a very dim notion, is the best illustration of such historical uniqueness. Such a historico-spiritual attitude is not fossilization of the national consciousness. It exhibits rather a peculiarity in the time awareness. Time is interwoven with eternity. Change and persistence, becoming and identical selfhood, form the background against which Jewish history must be seen.[1] Both the dawn of history and *aharit ha-yamim* ("the end of days") constitute for us historical realities. For us there always exists an everlasting past and a future actualized in prospect.

---

1. Maimonides' famous emphatic formulation (*Mishneh Torah, Hilkhot Hametz u-Matzah* 7:6) about the Jew at the Passover seder – "In every generation a person must show himself as if he himself went out now from the bondage in Egypt" – underscores this time awareness. Even when Maimonides offers step-by-step instructions for conducting the Passover seder in chapter 8, he presents it as if the Paschal lamb were a current reality; the present inability to offer the sacrifice is mentioned in one sentence (8:8). [See the Rav's parallel discussion in *Ish ha-Halakhah*, pp. 33–34. ed.]

The Historical Dimension of Charismatic Man

In this sense do I ascribe historicity to the charismatic personality. The charismatic person entering into a covenant with God and getting involved in a peculiar sort of history, in which both God and man appear, acquires historical constancy. I mean by this: Jewish historical persistence is based upon the divine performance. If God is drawn into the historical cycle, then some kind of identical selfhood, an unchanging identity, must be present. To be sure, there is change insofar as history expresses human deeds. Yet there must be eternal identity and selfhood, for God confined Himself within this historical occurrence. In consequence, the charismatic personality develops the awareness of historical persistence and continuity. Let us inquire into the life of the father of our nation.

> And the Lord said to Abraham, after Lot was separated from him, "Lift up now your eyes, and look from the place where you are, northward and southward, eastward and westward: for all the land which you see, to you will I give it, and to your seed forever.... Arise, walk through the land in the length of it and in the breadth of it, for I will give it to you" (Gen. 13:14–15, 17).

> I am the Lord who brought you out of Ur Kasdim, to give you this land to inherit it (15:7).

A question arises immediately. Abraham never took possession of the land and he never exercised any dominion over it. How could God promise him the land without fulfilling his words? God emphasized *lekha etnennah u-le-zar'ekha*: "I shall give the land to you (in person) and to your children" (13:15).

The answer to this question we find in Exodus.

> And I have also established My covenant with them, to give them the land of Canaan, the land of their sojournings, in which they sojourned (Ex. 6:4).

> And I will bring you into the land, which I swore to give to
> Abraham, to Isaac and to Jacob; and I will give it to you for
> a heritage: I am the Lord (Ex. 6:8).

The oath was not fulfilled during the lifetime of the patriarchs. It
came true many centuries later, when the children of Abraham,
Isaac and Jacob conquered the Land of Canaan. And yet the land
was specifically given to Abraham. Apparently, the words "to you
will I give it, and to your seed" express one thought: I shall give
the land to you *by having your children inherit it.* The realization
of the promise will occur on a historical level, on which the dead
and the living form one community and temporal instance loses
its meaning. Abraham will acquire the land through a conquest
hundreds of years later. Is this nonsense? Under no circumstances.
The charismatic personality is history-minded, future-anticipating
and future-experiencing. There is a quasi-mystical communion
between him and his descendants. The charismatic community
is again historically conscious, the past reliving and integrating
itself with the chosen individual who founded the nation.

The continuity-identity aspect of historical experience comes
to the fore. Abraham projects his existence upon a historical
background and introduces it into the everlasting community,
into a mysterious future, reaching out beyond the confines of its
natural existence. There is an act of self-transcendence. Abraham
exceeds the boundary line of individual, temporal existence and
reaches out into the open unlimited spaces of historical existence.
Abraham immortalizes himself in the continuous historical series
which he sponsored. He lives in the community and in the covenant. If I may use a mystical term, I would say that the historical
covenant community is the continuous incarnation of its father.
There is an "eternal" migration of the charismatic soul throughout
all phases of historical realization.

However, this unique appearance of the charismatic personality requires no mystical metaphors for its elucidation. It can easily
be explained by introducing ethical aspects. The universality of the

personality is an ethical performance. By discerning the moral law and with it the God of morality, the charismatic person realizes that the realization of the moral goal is not to be found within the bounds of an individual life span. The individual may contribute a great deal to the fulfillment of the ethical ideal, yet he can never attain it. A moral telos is *gradually* realized in a historical process.

That is why the charismatic person organizes a community, a medium which is guided by the vision of the founder. *Berit* is synonymous with *berit olam* – "eternal covenant." Covenant and eternity are identical. Yet the charismatic personality dedicates itself to the future, to the *aharit ha-yamim*, the end of days, to that wonderful moment when the vision will have become a "factum." He transplants his existence into that of the historical process. He identifies with its separate phases. He casts his personality into the continuum of historical fulfillment. He plans for the distant future, lives it through and pre-experiences its anticipated reality. He sees his ideal stature on a visionary level at the end of time, when all dreams will have been realized. He measures his imaginary personality with the real one which is to be found on the concrete historical level and tries to bridge the gap by establishing communion between the concrete world and the anticipated.

> And when the sun was going down, a deep sleep fell upon Abram; and lo, a horror of great darkness fell upon him. And He said to Abram, "Know surely that your seed shall be a stranger in a land that is not theirs; and they shall afflict them for four hundred years...." And it came to pass, that, when the sun went down... (Gen. 15:12–17).

This scene, as described in the Bible, fully conveys the experience of the charismatic person. The bondage of Israel in Egypt was not only predicted but illustrated and visualized. Abraham actually came into contact with the future sorrows and miseries of his children. He was overwhelmed by a vivid, sensuous awareness, which reached the intensity of real pain and suffering: a horror of great darkness fell upon him. The woes and agony of many years were condensed into a single moment. In an instant he went through the oppression, fear and uncertainty. For whatever would be inflicted upon his offspring was brought to him in its full impact and vigor. Sympathetic coexistence with countless future generations, confederacy with the unborn and anticipation of the wholeness of historical realization are the basic traits of the charismatic historical personality.

The children of Abraham are called Israel, after the last patriarch, Jacob. Why? Because there is continuity and identity of existence throughout the ages.

I will go down with you into Egypt, and I will also surely bring you up again (Gen. 46:4).

We understand the first half of the prophecy: "I will go down with you into Egypt." Yet the last part of the sentence does not make sense. God left Egypt with the myriads of the Children of Israel hundreds of years later. However, Moses' exodus is considered as if it were Jacob's personal triumph – "I will also surely bring you up again." God went out of Egypt with Jacob, although the latter had been dead for hundreds of years. What is the solution of this mystery? The historical personality answers our problem. As a natural being, as an individual who represents his genus, the charismatic personality is subject to a biological process of life which ends in death. Adam, as the archetype of such a personality, was mortal. The historical Abraham as a historical personality attained immortality. Yet Abraham did not conquer death in the metaphysical, transcendental sense. His immortality is through and through *historical*; immortality which consists in the charismatic proximity to a distant future and closeness to a remote past. Immortal is the personality which, incarnated in anticipation of the multitude of a non-existent group, is in turn incarnated by that group in retrospect. God reached a covenant with Abraham – not Abraham as a natural individual, one of many, but Abraham as a historical personality, now represented by the one Abraham of Beersheba, now as a collective, a clan, a people, a nation.

The covenant with Israel is not a new agreement reached by God with a nation but just the old treaty agreed upon by Him and Abraham. God emphasized this time and again in his revelation to Moses:

> I am the God of your father, the God of Abraham, the God of Isaac and the God of Jacob (Ex. 3:6).

> And I have also established My covenant with them, to give them the land of Canaan, the land of their sojournings... and I have remembered My covenant (Ex. 6:4–5).

He is not an alien God whom Moses meets, and through Moses, Israel. He is the God of the fathers.[2] However, it is not the natural, genealogical continuation that makes Him the God of Israel, but

---

2. According to the "Kenite" hypothesis of Biblical scholars, *Havayah* was unknown to Israel until then, being a tribal God of the Kenites, and Moses had discovered this God at his seat of worship on Sinai. But as Buber amply shows (*Moses*, pp. 42 ff.), this assumption is false. *Havayah* is the God of the patriarchs. We identify Him by the same unique relationship to His chosen group: entanglement in its historical destiny. God does not retreat into His transcendence, sending His people into the wilderness, but wanders with them. Of course the Bible critics support their thesis with the characteristic question of Moses "...and I shall say to them, the God of your fathers has sent me to you; and they shall say to me, *mah shemo?* ['What is His name?']" (Ex. 3:13). How is it possible, they contend, that Israel would not know the name of their paternal God. Yet Maimonides (*Guide of the Perplexed* 1:63–64) already noticed that the question in Hebrew *Mah shemo?* refers not to the phonetization of His name but to the interpretation. Buber (p. 48) quotes as an instance the question the "man" put up to Jacob "What is your name? And he said, 'Jacob'" (Gen. 32:28). He was not interested in the euphony of "Ya'akov" but rather in its eidetic content: "Thy name shall be called no more Ya'akov, but Yisrael; for you have contended with God and with men, and have prevailed" (Gen. 32:29). This was not a phonetic change, but a metaphysico-historical one. The heel-sneaker became a master, a victor.

historical continuity, which spells identity. Once again God makes His great demands of His men, soliciting and promising, re-establishing the old covenant with them. But now He no longer turns to a single Abraham, but to a people, collective-Abraham, and that people's existence is shared by God, in the same manner as he was involved in the adventures of the straying Syrian. The Abraham personality is recreated and reincarnated and relived time and again. There is only one covenant, that of the patriarchs:

> Then will I remember My covenant with Jacob, and also My covenant with Isaac, and also My covenant with Abraham will I remember; and I will remember the land (Lev. 26:42).

The name *Ehyeh* ("I will be") which God reveals to Moses at the burning bush (Ex. 3:14) conveys an identical idea: I am and remain present; not merely sometime and somewhere but in every now and in every here (Buber, *Moses*, p. 52). Why? Because I am

---

The same is true of Moses' question, as Buber shows on p. 51. The Jews will ask not after a mere etymologico-phonetic name, but will desire to apprehend the nature of the God of their fathers. How can we make use of His name? How shall we understand Him? The horrible experience of oppression put new doubts in their minds as to the God of their fathers. They have never heard of Him, and He had never intervened in their behalf. Let us not forget that the magical concept of divinity always points at the possibility of evoking and invoking him at certain intervals when man must receive supernatural assistance. The Jews probably tried to summon their God and to call Him forth many a time and He did not answer their call. The Jew of Egypt could not comprehend a God who cannot be invoked in moments of need.

The answer which was given to Moses constitutes a central thought in our philosophy. God has been present and will be present. There is no need for magical invocation and evocation (Buber, p. 50). God is entangled in your destiny, but there is historical necessity and evolutionary phases, which must take their course. There is no need to invoke divine assistance. Judaism is a covenant religion and as such it always presupposes divine interference with and involvement in the historical occurrence. Intimacy with God, not magical invocation, is the maxim. *Ehyeh asher Ehyeh* – "I am wherever I am" (Ex. 3:14). Magical formulas are futile.

entangled in the historical occurrence; I co-participate in the historical drama on account of My covenant with their fathers, whom Israel embodies now. The *Ehyeh* of God is *eo ipso* the assurance for the *Ehyeh* of the charismatic personality, whose destiny is interwoven with divine presence and sympathy and who affiliated himself with his fellow God-wanderer. Covenant existence is historical existence in its full uniqueness; existence in a present in which future and past converge. Covenant reality is a pluralistic one insofar as it is demonstrated by a multitude of individual realities. Yet it is at the same time monistic insofar as one existence expresses itself through all those existences. Israel is a people, as well as the patriarch. We use it both in plural and in singular. *Benei Yisrael* ("the Children of Israel") and Israel have an identical connotation: the children of Israel through whom Israel survives the fate of the natural being. The natural ego is assimilated into an individualistic ego who lived at the dawn of history. The nation is as unique and as lonely as their father-shepherd Abraham was. The people relive his life, of course in a different environment yet in identical situations. The uniqueness of such a historical existence consists in projecting a present onto a mystical future, and vice-versa in tying it in with a dim past.

Hegel's famous definition, that the historicity of a group is determined by its historical memory, does not do justice to the problem of Jewish history. Mere remembrance – a psychological phenomenon – does not suffice. Our historicity is expressed in covenant constancy and identity. Not only do we remember our past but we relive and re-experience it. Moreover, the past asserts itself in the present. Yet, both past and present manifest themselves in an act of anticipation and expectation of a future. Our memory is the living covenant, recreating and reincarnating metaphysical retrospective experience, which is at the same time the prophetic vision of the end of the days. The identity of Abraham has not been lost throughout the generations. The identity of the Messiah has not been erased from our historical consciousness in spite of its visionary reality.

Prophetic and Ethical Memory

Historical belonging, which binds the individual with an array of past and future generations, is the basis of Jewish historical understanding, although no history can afford to free itself from this burden. Yet it is not an act of metaphysical reincarnation as the Lurianic school asserted, nor is it a mere psychological continuity of a collective memory. It asserts itself in two unique attitudes: (1) in a prophetic memory – in the God-man encounter; (2) in an ethical memory – in the consciousness of historical duty assumed by the charismatic personality.

The first attitude finds expression in the perennial prophetic consciousness. God spoke not only to the founder of the nation but to us as well. "Has the Lord indeed spoken only with Moses? Has He not spoken also with us?" (Num. 12:2). The ablative case ("has He not?") emphasizes not so much the actual sensuous apprehension of the divine word by other persons but its intentional meaning, its directedness and its dynamic historical force. God's word *belongs* to the entire community. Why? Because the God of Abraham, Isaac and Jacob addresses Himself to His fellow shepherds of old, to Israel as a nation, to the charismatic personality which shines through the multitude. Moses is just the agent who transmits the word. Prophecy as such is not Moses' exclusively.

> ...seeing all the congregation are holy, every one of them,
> and the Lord is among them (Num. 16:3).

Yet the divine word is not the temporal, one-timely phonos (sound) but the eternal divine logos (word, thought, idea, will), which was conveyed to the charismatic group and which became historical reality.

> Only take heed to yourself, and keep your soul diligently, lest
> you forget the things which your eyes have seen, and lest they
> depart from your hearts all the days of your life: but teach

them to your sons, and your sons' sons – the day that you
stood before the Lord your God in Horeb (Deut. 4:9–10).

The commandment of *zekhirat ma'amad Har Sinai*, remembering
the revelation at Sinai, signifies a perennial living experience; that
day has never come to an end. Likewise the law that "in every
generation a person must see himself as if he left Egypt" means
the historical integration with a distant past, the act of reliving
and re-experiencing it. Let us not forget that the act of *zekher* is
applied not only to man but the God as well. Basically, it is a divine
attribute; humans just borrowed it.

> And God remembered (*va-yizkor*) Noah, and every living thing,
> and all the cattle that was with him in the ark (Gen. 8:1).

> And the Lord visited (*pakad*) Sarah (Gen. 21:1).

> I have surely visited (*pakod pakadeti*) you (Ex. 3:16).

> Then will I remember (*ve-zakharti*) My covenant with Jacob,
> and also My covenant with Isaac…(Lev. 26:42).

The Halakhah formulated *Birkat Zikhronot* (the blessing of "remembrance") in the *Musaf* prayer for Rosh Ha-Shanah and coined
a unique blessing: *zokher ha-berit* ("who remembers the covenant"), formulated in the present tense. *Zikkaron* as a divine
attribute cannot connote any psychological process. It must be
understood under a transcendental aspect. *Zikkaron* as an attribute of God denotes not remembrance of the past but its presence,
its perennial existence and everlasting reality. Time does not flow
on, but comes to a standstill. Past, present and future are interwoven. The covenant with Abraham does not lie in a dead past
but in a living present; *zokher ha-berit* describes the actuality and
reality of the *berit*.

As a consequence of the perennial *berit* consciousness, we

may speak of a historical ethical memory. Agreements entered into, obligations assumed, promises made, objectives formulated by the father of the nation are valid and binding for the charismatic group. We remember the ethical duty contained in the covenant. Again, this is not just simple remembrance; it is rather a re-acceptance, a re-experience. We assumed our duties through Abraham and Moses. They represented us, and we in turn represent them.

Analyzing this topic in somewhat greater detail, we shall discover another – familiar – aspect, namely, that of ethical solidarity and co-responsibility. Historical sin, punishment and reward are original Jewish ideas. Just as the natural individual is responsible for his own deeds, the group bears responsibility for the sins of the past. This is not to be equated with hereditary sin. The latter, as developed by Christian thinkers, is a metaphysical, objective quality, inherent in human natural existence. Historical sin signifies a historical category, which asserts itself in historical continuity. The individual is not guilty of sins perpetrated by past generations. The historical group is responsible for historical errors and sins committed by the fathers, because the latter repeat their existence in their descendants.

> And they shall confess their iniquity, and the iniquity of their fathers, with their trespass which they trespassed against Me (Lev. 26:40).

The authentic historical figure suffers for the past and fully relives it. As was emphasized above, the amalgamating force, which unites generations throughout the ages, is the ethical ideal, which can never be fulfilled. This ideal discovered by the charismatic personality, to whose realization he dedicated himself and his clan, perpetuates the existence of the founder. As long as the ideal has not materialized, the charismatic personality cannot die, for its life was given to its fulfillment. The clan or nation, which carries on, identifies itself in a prelogical feeling with its father.

The first concept of immortality as coined by Judaism is the continuation of a historical existence throughout the ages. It differs from transcendental immortality insofar as the deceased person does not lead an isolated, separate existence in a transcendental world. The identity persists on a level of concrete reality disguised as a people. It asserts itself in the consciousness of the many, who trace their roots to the one. Yet metaphysical immortality is based upon historical immortality. Whoever does not identify himself with the historical ego and remains on the natural level cannot attain immortality. The first conquest of death takes place in the realm of history.

Worthy of note is the following Rabbinic statement (*Sanhedrin* 90b):

> From where do we know that [belief in] the resurrection of the dead is [a concept] in the Torah? As it says, "And you shall give of it the Lord's gift [*terumah*] to Aaron the priest" (Num. 18:28). Is Aaron alive forever? Is it possible to give *terumah* to someone who did not enter the Land of Israel? Rather, this teaches that he [Aaron] will live again, and Israel will give him their *terumah*. From here [we learn] that the resurrection of the dead is [a concept] in the Torah.... We learned in a *beraita*: Rav Simai said: From where do we know that [belief in] the resurrection of the dead is [a concept] in the Torah? As it is said: "And I have also established my covenant with them [the patriarchs], to give them the land of Canaan, the land of their sojournings" (Ex. 6:4). It does not say "To you" [i.e., the descendants] but "to them" [i.e., the patriarchs] – From here [we learn] that the resurrection of the dead is [a concept] in the Torah.

Our Rabbis singled out the unique Biblical usage of the name of the founder (Aaron or Abraham) for the identification of the group, and concluded from that that the founder is immortal. The argument is comprehensible only when we consider it from the viewpoint of historical perpetuation. The land was promised to Abraham, *terumah* to Aaron. The realization of this promise did not occur in their lifetimes but many years later and yet the word of God came true. Why? Because the founder continues his existence throughout the history of his group. Whatever is realized in the cause of the historical occurrence is to be understood as a personal attainment of the founder.

CHAPTER 10

Charismatic Man as Prophet: Moses

The idea of the covenant inherently denotes two separate stages: a great promise and vision, during which the free charismatic personality discovers God and affiliates with Him, and a realization of that promise in a distant future. Promise lies at the threshold of the historical interim, fulfillment at the end. The two are separated by an interim period, after which the covenant finds its conclusion.

The "Interim" Period of the Covenant

What is the characteristic of the interim, of the long "between"? The apparent deterioration of the covenant. The covenant is always a revolutionary force that collides with the existing order of things. There is a perennial conflict between the historical-covenant motivation and historical immediacy. The concrete historical situation contradicts the great promise and stamps it as absurd and illogical. The covenant appears to oppose historical regularity and continuity. The paradoxical nature of the promise, its logic of the absurd, comes to the surface during the "interim."

The history of the patriarchs is replete with examples of this: Abraham within his own household encountered opposition (Ishmael, the sons of Keturah) and conflict. In Isaac the covenant runs into opposition: his two sons Esau and Jacob represent the eternal conflict between a historical natural reality and a covenantal charismatic mission. The history of our patriarchs points time and again to the moments of tension that developed within the chosen clan in regard to the covenant. The charismatic personality becomes entangled in numerous exigencies, which complicate his task and render the covenant ludicrous. The vision of the great fulfillment recedes into the shadow of absurdity, and concrete historical forces triumph over a prophecy and a testament. The emigration of Jacob's family to Egypt and its subsequent enslavement marked the full reversal of the covenant. All promises seemed to be refuted and the fellowship of man and God dissolved. Apparently the antithesis is inherent in the covenant itself. The self-negation of the covenant must precede its fulfillment. We may characterize the covenant in almost Hegelian terms.

The unfolding of the covenant forces occurs along dialectical lines. Within the covenant-clan itself the antithesis grows to tremendous proportions and begins to cast its shadow upon the great promise. Yet the antinomic motif is not powerful enough to bring the covenant to complete failure. It only succeeds in introducing a historical crisis. At the very moment at which the great message is about to lose its meaning, the fulfillment matures. We may speak of a historical triad: *thesis* – promise and the formation of the God-man confederacy; *antithesis* – the interim, at which the covenant negates and drives itself ad absurdum; *synthesis* – the release of historical tension and fulfillment.

Let us inquire into this synthesis. What is the nature of the thesis and the antithesis?

The charismatic personality establishes a covenant with his God and through it raises himself to a new level of existence, the historico-teleological. Yet, the charismatic personality or clan is attached to the moorings of an organized, regular and monotonous reality. The level of natural, concrete existence cannot be ignored. "The central figures of the Bible are not, as in so many hero-tales, merged in or amalgamated with persons belonging to mere mythology; the data regarding their lives have not been interwoven with stories of the gods. Here all the glorification is dedicated solely to the God who brings about the events. The human being acting under God's orders is portrayed in all his untransfigured humanity" (Buber, *Moses*, p. 17). Hence he acts under normal circumstances and is subject to the unalterable laws of a natural existence, to all the indifferent, purposeless forces of a self-sufficient, blind being, which does not recognize covenant motifs and charismatic patterns in history.

Indeed, the chosen clan itself is heterogeneous: charismatic-historical and natural-orgiastic. Two orders, which are mutually exclusive, run parallel to each other. The antithesis is an integral part of the covenant, which does not withdraw the human being from a human existence. The human being as such contradicts the great promise and denies the terms of the covenant. The charismatic motivation clashes with the orgiastic tendencies. The antithesis is the natural man himself.

In what does the synthesis of fulfillment consist? At this point a new person emerges in the historical arena: Moses; with his coming, the drama of realization begins.

Abraham vs. Moses

At first glance, there are quite a few similarities between the lives of Abraham and Moses. (1) Both were reared in an urban society, controlled by a central state authority. Both experience the full impact of a political and religious tyranny, of a magical technic. (2) Both flee from a stabilized civilization into the midst of a fluid nomadic society: Abraham – because of a divine commandment; Moses – under the pressure of political circumstances. Both go into an alien environment, culturally inferior to the one they fled. Both become fully equipped and grow to their full stature in steppes of pasture land and desert sands. Both engage in the trade of shepherd. The builders of a nation must tend the flocks of innocent sheep and goats. (3) Both revolted against human conventions and man-made institutions and discovered the genuine, original law of morality. The old Hebrew encounter of prophet versus king is characteristic of both. (4) Both experience the numinous encounter with God, without which a religious life can hardly be comprehensible.

Yet there is a distinct difference between Abraham and Moses. Abraham, upon discovering the moral law, and upon severing himself from a legalistic, magical society, discovers also the God of morality. His anarchic outcry against a ruthless state leads him to a free, lonely God, without suddenly encountering a transcendent deity. Moses discovered the moral law when he went out to his brethren and defended a helpless slave against the brutal attack of an Egyptian master. Yet this very morality did not disclose to him new historical horizons. We are not aware of any personal metamorphosis in Moses due to his bitter experience with his mother civilization. In spite of that episode, he remained the elegant courtier. As the daughters of Jethro tell their father:

An Egyptian man (*mitzri*) delivered us out of the hand of the shepherds (Ex. 2:19).

Moses did not renounce his affiliation with the Egyptian society. Not until he was well engrossed in his mission, which resulted from the majestic scene of the burning bush, did our redeemer realize the change which had come upon him.

That is the crux of the matter, and that is why the story of Moses is diametrically opposed to that of Abraham. While the father of the nation voluntarily undertakes a historical mission without experiencing any duress or compulsion, the redeemer is forced by apocalyptic command into a historical situation. He did not discover God; nor did he select Him or the moral law. The apocalyptic revelation surprised him and took him prisoner. He encountered apocalyptic necessity. God commanded, and he tried to resist, without success. What does this resistance signify? The rampancy of the antithetic forces. Even the redeemer himself realized the greatness of the event and the truthfulness of the covenant. Moses himself was a child of the interim period. What kind of compulsion did God use? Of course, not His cosmic power; He did not apply force to Moses. He introduced Himself not as the Autocrat of the universe but as the God of Moses' fathers, as the God of the covenant. The necessity which Moses encountered was of a historical nature – the historical need.

> And I have also established My covenant with them, to give them the land of Canaan, the land of their sojournings (Ex. 6:4).

Of course, the moment of sympathy comes up in the dialogue from time to time. However, it plays a secondary role.

> And I have also heard the groaning of the children of Israel, kept in bondage by Egypt (6:5).

The central theme is the covenant-idea *va-ezkor et beriti*, "I have remembered My covenant." God acts here in the role of a co-participant in the historical destiny of His confederates and is duty-bound to bring the covenant to full realization. There is no other alternative. The promise must come true regardless of the willingness of the chosen clan. Moses, as a natural man, offers resistance to the logic of the absurd. Yet God does not use natural power to make Moses obey, but argues with him about historical inevitability and necessity. Moses argues, "But, behold, they will not believe me, nor hearken to my voice: for they will say: the Lord has not appeared to you" (Ex. 4:1). He emphasizes the inadequacy of the people to raise themselves to the heights of faith (the close association with God through the interim period). God endows him with supernatural power to perform certain miraculous deeds. Moses attains here a new stature.

The Role of "Agent"
Moses introduces a new motif into the God-man fellowship,

namely, that of *shelihut* – agency. He becomes the divine angel who acts on behalf of God and represents Him.

> ...and sent an angel, and brought us out of Egypt (Num. 20:16).

The angelic role – that is to say, the role of agent – of the charismatic personality was assigned for the first time to Moses. Abraham was never charged with such a task. He never represented God as His emissary. No divine power was delegated to him. He discovered God, was quite intimate with Him, yet had no right to act as His spokesman. Whatever he preached he did on his own behalf. The angelic mission was denied to him. When he instructed his family, he did not act as a divine representative. Moses was the first person to receive the word from God: "Come now therefore, and I will send you to Pharaoh" (Ex. 3:10). The idea of the prophetic speech was introduced into the world: *ko amar Hashem* – "thus says the Lord." Man appears as an agent of God.[1]

The apostolic idea is denotative of a new aspect in the covenant. The covenant not only involves God in the human historical occurrence of His chosen people but draws man into the historical divine performance. God wanders with His chosen friend or friends, and shares in their destiny. Man coordinates his activities with divine planning and co-participates in the realization of the great promise. There is no division of duties within the contractual bounds. There is a cooperative effort on both parts: divine and human. Man is implicated in the divine scheme of things and joins God in carrying out the historical task. God worked through Moses in order to introduce man into the sphere of historical creativeness. Let man himself attempt to realize the covenant. Let this realization occur within the bounds of human activity.

---

1. Christianity could not solve the meaning of divine agency and converted God's apostle into a deity. We, however, refused to do so. Moses remained a human figure in all his idiosyncrasies. The angelic task is human through and through.

Moses embodies both ends of the covenant, the divine and the human. He is God's emissary to Israel and at the same time he is the spokesman of Israel before God. The covenant assures man not only of divine companionship but of divine attributes. There is a merger of tasks, of performances. God participates in the interim phases of covenant self-negation; man shares the divine execution of covenant realization. The messianic hope is based upon this aspect. Man acts as a divine agent and redeems himself.

Why did God merge His task with the human?

God acts not only under a dynamic aspect but under a pedagogical one as well. He delegates power and responsibility to man in order to raise him to a new level of personalistic existence. He lends His power to the apostolic personality.

In the interim period, the conflict between the natural human order and the charismatic historic order asserts itself. Under the impact of antithetic natural inevitability, the covenant is brought to a critical point; its fulfillment becomes almost impossible. The realization of the promise spells the great historical synthesis in the dialectical process, the reconciliation of the natural and historical orders, the assimilation of the esthetic orgiastic personality into the charismatic-historical. Redemption means the great miraculous act of rendering human reality commensurable in all its manifestations, particularly in its historic-teleological and orgiastic-esthetic orders. In other words: we will witness the triumph of the ethical over the esthetic, the assertion of the charismatic-meaningful over the indifferent-meaningless. The logic of the absurd that characterized the antithetic period of self-negation, when all seemed hopeless, becomes the logic of the reasonable during the synthesis performance. Man himself is chosen to carry out the task of harmonization of those two orders.

First, God appoints man as His agent, His plenipotentiary. In the capacity of a redeemer, man must reconcile both opposing forces and emerge as a harmonious personality. The split brought about by Adam must be healed. The dual personality, consisting of a genuine ethical existence and an adopted orgiastic one, must be raised to the level of harmony. Cosmic law and moral law become identical as originally intended; ethical designs are woven into the cosmic texture, and a natural existence is the background against which the ethos should be seen. Faith in the inevitable fulfillment of the covenant is unshakable, a passionate, optimistic faith in the ultimate sensibility and meaningfulness of the historical process. It is, inherently, a paradoxical faith; in spite of the horrifying length and monotony of the antithetic interim, the synthesis must finally come true.

In this respect, the redeemer does not embody all the qualities of the charismatic personality. The latter dedicates itself to God without going through any mental agony and without being pulled by conflicting forces. The charismatic person is not torn by internal strife nor does he experience a dual existence and the misery of ontic incongruity. His career is that of a harmonious personality marked by gradual development and growth; the moment of tension is almost non-existent in his relationship to his God. He discovered Him and he follows Him without fleeing and retreating. The charismatic person stands at the threshold of covenant historicity, before the antithetic interim begins to assert itself.

Moses, by contrast, is a child of antithetic times, of interim indifference. In contradistinction to the father of the nation, his mental and spiritual development follows a zig-zag line. Moses, at the outset, was by far not as perfect as Abraham. He lacked initiative; he resisted God's command; he did not experience the historical, fateful urge and drive to undertake the impossible. He did not display the unequivocal, resolute, fiery faith in the fulfillment of the covenant. He had to go through the purging and purifying experiences of the exodus, the Sinaitic revelation, the golden calf episode and his lonely rendezvous with God on the top of the rock before he could attain the great miraculous human stature. Yet his personality was shaped and developed through an almost superhuman effort; its path was tortuous. Moses' greatness was not of a charismatic nature; he belonged to the interim period, struggling with his own personality as he re-educated, re-trained and re-formed himself. If Abraham's life was one of a constructive effort, Moses' was of a re-constructive. He was a self-made historical personality. An ethical passional will triumphed over an indifferent antithetic nature. He subjected himself to a covenantal historical reality and actually forced his natural existence into the pre-arranged scheme of things. That is why Moses' prophetic career began with an apocalyptic experience. For had providence waited for Moses, the shepherd would never have found God. The voice coming forth from the burning bush and Moses' resistance symbolize the clash of the thesis with antithesis. The final *reformation* of Moses embodies the synthesis of redemption.

Redemption's Miracle: The Merger of the Historical and the Natural

How did this work of reformation-redemption proceed? Here the miracle appears. The supernatural miracle is not very welcome in the covenant society. We prefer the regular flow of life. The Halakhah is completely integrated with the natural process. It never takes cognizance of any causalistic anomalies. Yet the central theme of the exodus tale is the miracle.

What is a miracle in Judaism? The word "miracle" in Hebrew does not possess the connotation of the supernatural. It has never been placed on a transcendental level. "Miracle" (*pele, nes*) describes only an outstanding event which causes amazement. A turning point in history is always a miracle, for it commands attention as an event which intervened fatefully in the formation of that group or that individual. As we read the story of the exodus from Egypt, we are impressed by the distinct tendency of the Bible to relate the events in natural terms. The frogs came out of the river when the Nile rose, the wind brought the locusts and split the sea. All archaeologists agree that the plagues as depicted by the Bible are very closely related to the geographical and climatic conditions that prevail in Egypt. Behind the passages in the Bible we may discern a distinct intention to describe the plagues as naturally as possible. The Bible never emphasizes the unnaturalness of the events; only its intensity and force are emphasized. The reason for that is obvious. A philosophy which considers the world-drama as a fixed, mechanical process governed by an unintelligent, indifferent principle, may regard the miracle as a supernatural transcendental phenomenon which does not fit into the causalistic, meaningless monotony. Israel, however, who looked upon the universal occurrence as the continuous realization of a divine ethical will embedded into dead and live matter, could never classify the miracle as something unique and incomprehensible. Both natural monotony and the surprising element in nature express God's word. Both are regular, lawful phenomena; both can be traced to an identical source. In the famous Psalm 104, *Barkhi nafshi* ("My soul will bless"), the psalmist describes the most elementary natural phenomena like the propagation of light in terms of wonder and astonishment – no different from Moses' Song at the Sea. The whole cosmos unfolds itself as a miraculous revelation of God. The demarcation line between revelation and nature is almost non-existent!

In what, then, does the uniqueness of the miracle assert itself? In the correspondence of the natural and historical orders. The miracle does not destroy the objective scientific nexus in itself, it only combines natural dynamics and historical purposefulness. Had the plague of the firstborn, for instance, occurred a year before or after the exodus, it would not have been termed "with a strong hand" (*be-yad hazakah*). Why? God would have been instrumental in a natural children's plague. Yet God acts just as the world ruler. On the night of Passover He appeared as the God of the cosmos acting along historical patterns. The intervention of nature in the historical process is a miracle. Whether God planned that history adjust itself to natural catastrophes or, vice versa, He commands nature to cooperate with the historical forces, is irrelevant. Miracle is simply a natural event which causes a historical metamorphosis. Whenever history is transfigured under the impact of cosmic dynamics, we encounter a miracle.

We see that the Torah incessantly stresses the miraculous when reflecting on or recalling the redemption from Egypt:

And that you may tell in the ears of your son, and of your son's son, what things I have done in Egypt (Ex. 10:2).

For by strength of hand the Lord brought us forth out of Egypt (Ex. 13:16).

And it came to pass when Pharaoh would hardly let us go, that the Lord slew all the firstborn in the land of Egypt (Ex. 13:15).

The great trials which your eyes have seen, the signs, and those great miracles (Deut. 29:2).

And the Lord brought us out of Egypt with a mighty hand, and with an outstretched arm, and with great terribleness, and with signs and with wonders (Deut. 26:8).

When the antithesis reached its climax and the historicity of the covenant came to a critical point, God wanted to demonstrate the unalterable necessity inherent in the charismatic historical occurrence. It cannot and will not be curtailed by any natural forces. If the need arises, the covenant will become a factum, even if other factors will have to be altered because of that. Miracle expresses the idea that whenever the covenant comes to a crisis in its eternal struggle with the forces of indifference, the historical motives will overcome the opposition of a cruel reality. Historical values will emerge victorious from the clash with actual forces, which during the interim seemed to run contrary to the vision of realization. This faith is rooted in our identification of both realms – the historical and the universal. Human intelligence has separated them from each other. Yet in the divine infinite consciousness, the cosmic law is at the same time a moral law and morality is natural. "I form the light, and create darkness: I make peace, and create evil" (Isa. 45:7). Light and darkness – two natural phenomena, and peace and evil – two ethical concepts, are correlated. Moreover, they merge together into one divine creation. God reveals Himself through the cosmos in the natural law and through the ethical universe. The unity of God warrants the unity of both orders: the natural and the moral.

This is a commonplace in the prophetic world formula and needs no further elucidation. However, as we explained in detail in the second part of this essay, man has introduced a cleavage between the natural and ethical orders. The ethical personality with its drive toward sympathetic coexistence suddenly encountered the esthetic, orgiastic personality with all its demonism. The genuine existence clashed with a pseudo-existence, and man surrendered to the demonic forces. Of course, his surrender was not complete. The true personality retreated, yet did not accept defeat. Man developed a dual personality. The antithetic, self-negating quality is inherent in him. He clashes with himself, he struggles within his own existence, the experience of conflict is the very genuine expression of his primordial being. Self-denial is inherent in the most secret recesses of his spiritual reality. Human existence is dialectical, self-contradictory and self-neutralizing.

The charismatic personality overcomes this dichotomy, to a certain extent, by discovering the moral law and its author, the God of the cosmos. In Abraham we notice the longing for harmony. He addresses God both as the *shofet kol ha-aretz*, "Judge of the world" (Gen. 18:25) – the God of morality – and as *E-lokei ha-shamayim ve-lokei ha-aretz*, "God of the heavens and of the earth" (24:3) – the God of the cosmos. As soon as the charismatic person realized the identity of *mishpat* (justice) and the natural world order, he attained the desired synthesis. His personality reached the ideal unity of the ontos and the ethos, of the ethical and ontic motives. The covenant in itself is the daring attempt to overcome the tragic duality in human existence. The covenant expresses the absolute unity of both motives: cosmic dynamics and morality.

The covenant, however, restoring unity to human personality, contains its own antithesis. Whereas the orgiastic-esthetic existence casts off the ethical authority and begins to revolt against the moral order, the antithetic forces in history are themselves the demonic assertion of historical reality, which come to the surface again within the covenant-society. Demonic versus ethical existence is the leitmotif of the interim period. The battle is a drawn-out affair. The demonic dynamics drive the covenant to the point of absurdity. Only then does the phase of realization begin. Yet fulfillment of the covenant means realization of the human personality, the merger of the biological and ethical motivations. For our historical existence is not transcendental or supernatural, as many have attempted to philosophize. Our historical reality expresses full concreteness and this-worldliness. It is a natural reality, in which God is involved and which rises to historical heights. Historical and natural realities become coordinated, supplementary. The merger of both is the great aim.

> The wolf also shall dwell with the lamb, and the leopard shall lie down with the kid; and the calf and the young lion and the fatling together; and a little child shall lead them. And the cow and the bear shall feed: and their young ones shall lie down together: and the lion shall eat straw like an ox. And the sucking child shall play on the hole of the cobra, and the weaned child shall put his hand on the viper's nest. They shall not hurt nor destroy in all My holy mountain: for the earth shall be full of the knowledge of the Lord, as the waters cover the sea (Isa. 11:6–9).

In this messianic idyll, the prophet depicts in glowing colors the harmonious state that will prevail in nature. The biological being will not follow its orgiastic instincts; instead it will be guided by an ethical impulse. Nature will be hallowed, the animal in us will be sanctified. The demonic drive will be converted into an ethical motivation. The ethos and bios will cooperate and coexist. The words "and the lion shall eat straw like an ox" are remarkable. They allude to the primordial antediluvian state of things, when man and animal were cereal eaters. The biological being will not overstep the boundary line of its existence, will not reach out after something alien. In other words, *hamas* will disappear. "Violence shall no more be heard in your land" (Isa. 60:18). The great ideal is redemption of man and nature, the elevation of the natural level to the ethical one.

The interim period, at which the antithesis asserts itself, is marked by an intensification of the conflict between the two opposing forms of existence. The fulfillment-era is distinguished by the closing of the ontic gap and the reconciliation of the demonic and ethical personalities, of Adam and the serpent. "And the sucking child shall play on the hole of the cobra, and the weaned child shall put his hand on the viper's nest" is just the reversal of the divine curse "and I will put enmity between you and the woman, and between your seed and her seed" (Gen. 3:15).

The redeemer is God's emissary and brings about this marvelous state. Moses, the first redeemer, began the work; Messiah will complete it.

Imitatio Dei

The apostolic personality co-participates with God in the realization of the great promise, in performing a divine task. Thus the idea of *imitatio Dei* is born. Man is not satisfied with the mere role of being human and limiting himself within the scope of his finite tasks and duties. There is an act of self-transcendence on his part. Yet this daring attempt is quite different from the demonic self-transcendence which came to the fore with the original sin. There man exceeds the natural boundary line of his existence and reaches out for something alien and hostile to his natural existence. An act of treachery is involved in the non-natural attempt to exploit nature for the sake of an orgiastic-esthetic experience. In the apostolic transcending is implied a historical adventure. I am freeing myself from the concrete and natural in order to attain the historical, which is synonymous with the natural. While Adam stole secrets from nature in order to defeat its very plan and objective, Moses imposed upon it a new aspect – the historical – and made it cooperate with the new order. Moses actually reminded nature of its genuine purpose and primordial aspect. The natural and moral orders merge. Man begins to lead an ethical existence, because he coordinates with the ontic aspect of God. He becomes God's apostle on earth, who participates in the divine act of realization. First man was meant to exist and to experience his existence as morality. Later he betrayed Mother Nature and emerged as a dual personality, demonic and ethical. The former experiences existence under an esthetic aspect. The apostolic personality finds the solution to the problem of a dual existence. Man becomes God's companion and agent, rehabilitating himself by it. He begins to imitate God and finds consolation in the act of assimilating himself into a fellow-wanderer and executor of the divine will.

Expansion of the Covenant: "A Kingdom of Priests"

At this stage the royal personality appears.

The Bible critics, advocates of the "Kenite Hypothesis," claim that "If God had been the God of Israel even before Moses, a covenant would have been superfluous" (Buber, *Moses*, p. 42). The covenant concluded with the patriarchs would have been sufficient for the constitution of Israel's relationship with God. For this reason, they maintain, Israel and God did not hitherto know each other. Apparently, these scholars interpreted the covenant episode at Sinai as the conclusion of a *new* agreement. Yet, reading the chapters in Exodus which deal with the covenant, we do not discover that the Bible conceives it as something new. On the contrary, the narrative emphasizes the historical character of the occurrence. It never mentions that this was a surprise performance on the part of God.

The first divine message to Israel begins with the following words:

> ...this shall you say to the house of Jacob, and tell the children of Israel (Ex. 19:3).

He addresses Himself not to a new people, to strangers, but to the house of Jacob and to the children of Israel. A historical reference to an old bond of companionship is quite obvious. The middle part of the speech (the conditional part) –

> Now therefore, if you will obey My voice indeed, and keep My covenant, then you shall be My own treasure from among all peoples (v. 5) –

does not make a new offer of a covenant, but speaks of an old agreement which has been in existence for a long time. The only new element in this message is the closing sentence:

> …then you shall be My own treasure from among all peoples…and you shall be to Me a kingdom of priests, and a holy nation (19:5–6).

By observing the covenant, the people will be a unique treasure and a kingdom of priests and a holy nation. This promise is new. Abraham was never told of a *mamlekhet kohanim*, "a kingdom of priests." He was promised a great nation – "and I will make of you a great nation" (Gen. 12:2) – yet never was the future priestly role of his children mentioned. This indicates a new phase in the covenant; however, this does not convey to us the idea of an entirely new covenant. Even the second narrative of the covenant-conclusion in Exodus 24 –

> And he took the book of the covenant, and read in the hearing of the people: and they said, "All that the Lord has said we will do, and obey." And Moses took the blood, and sprinkled it on the people, and said, "Behold the blood of the covenant, which the Lord has made with you concerning all these words" (vv. 7–8) –

does not imply a new contractual relationship. It only refers to a new development, to the expansion of the covenant, the promulgation of new stipulations, laws and conditions. Yet the covenant as such is as old as Israel itself.

We may say that the new aspect in the Sinaitic covenant is the idea of *mamlekhet kohanim*, a "divine-human kingdom." God speaking from the flame had anticipated this hour:

> And I will take you to Me as a people, and I will be to you a God (Ex. 6:7).

Now He proclaims that the moment has come and the idea of the kingdom may be realized. What does it mean?

In Hebrew, the term *melekh*, king, has a twofold connotation:

(1) *Melekh* as a ruler or autocrat, who exercises control and power over something. In this sense, *malkhut,* kingship, is a cosmic category. The whole cosmic drama may be looked upon as the realization of a powerful, all-inclusive will. The whole relationship between God and His creation expresses royal dominion.

> The Lord reigns (*Hashem malakh*), He is clothed with majesty; the Lord is robed; He has girded Himself with strength: the world also is established, that it cannot be moved. Your throne is established of old: You are from everlasting. The floods have lifted up O Lord, the floods have lifted up their voice; the floods lift up their roaring. The Lord on high is mightier than the noise of many waters, than the mighty waves of the sea (Ps. 93:1–4).

The psalm depicts the cosmic dynamics in terms of *malkhut*. In most cases, the verb *m.l.kh.* is applied to cosmic dominion, or to His will as expressed in the law of nature. The noun *melekh*, in fact, is very seldom used in reference to God: e.g., "and He...as King forever" (Ps. 29:10).

(2) *Malkhut* and *melekh* as they denote a political concept:

God as a political ruler wielding power over human beings who accept His authority. God seen within the framework of the state is *melekh*, king. The old concept of *melekh* should be understood in a political sense. God is the king of a chosen society. We should not equate this rule with overlordship and autocracy. The divine kingdom is constitutionally regulated and freely accepted. The term covenant itself excludes any tyranny. The tyrant does not reach any contract with his subjects.

In order to achieve this phase, this notion of *malkhut*, God had to realize His great promise. For the granting of the status of a king to Him is a result of His companionship with Israel during the interim period. I always picture the proclamation of the divine kingdom at Sinai as the rewarding with a sovereign crown a beloved companion who guided to victory a revolutionary band during times of trial and sacrifice, when the whole movement was banned and persecuted. When all the promises came true and the elder of the clan faithfully fulfilled his mission, the grateful members grant their beloved leader-comrade royal power as a token of appreciation.

> And He was king in Jeshurun, when the heads of the people
> and the tribes of Israel were gathered together (Deut. 33:5).

God is a king *in* Israel, not *over* Israel (see 1 Sam. 19). His kingdom was established at the conclave of the elders of the people. In other words: God's kingdom was not imposed; He did not usurp power. It was granted to Him. His royal dominion is a covenant arrangement.

> …the Lord his God is with him, *u-teru'at melekh bo* – and
> the trumpet blast of the king *is among them* (Num. 23:21).

God is described as being a member of the group, a fellow-wanderer, a friend and comrade. There is no rule from above, transcendence, absolute supremacy, royal pride and inaccessibility.

In contrast with "The Lord reigns, He is clothed with majesty," which expresses cosmic dominion, God's kingdom in Israel is permeated with intimacy and closeness. Philo misunderstood this relationship and named the Judaic state a theocracy. The very idea of covenant contradicts the meaning of theocracy as an alien rule imposed upon a certain society. Instead I would suggest that the Hebrew term *teru'at melekh* should be understood as "theo-comradeship," or "theo-politeia," a God-man community; autocracy is excluded if *malkhut* is to be understood as a political concept.

At Sinai, the phase of realization began and with it the royal dominion of God. God as the cosmic ruler of the universe is not a king. God was known to Abraham either as fellow companion, who commands and leads, or as *E-lokei ha-shamayim ve-lokei ha-aretz*, the cosmic creator; He was never known as a king within a political society. For divine kingship is dependent upon the realization of the covenant.

Throughout the interim period, God was a fellow-wanderer, a co-martyr, a sympathetic companion; yet there was no kingdom. For the divine kingdom can only be realized when the historical order is reconciled with the natural. The proclamation of His royal dominion is *eo ipso* the rehabilitation of creation itself. In a world which is torn by inimical forces, the divine kingdom can never come true. The interim period is marked by divine cosmic dominion, by politico-historical retreat or, *kivyakhol,* divine passivity. God suffers with His chosen community. He is involved in their fateful experiences and waits with them for the realization of His own great promise. Politico-historically He remains inactive. He is committed to the cosmos but not to human society.

The triumph arrived with the covenant, and is associated with God's entry into human society, His emergence as a political ruler into the historical arena. The resumption of His political activity and creativity spelled the realization of the covenant. The God of Israel, *E-lokei Yisrael*, is the comrade-king of Israelite society. Moses discovered God under a historico-political attribute. When cosmic autocratism and historical kingship are fused – in other words, when the historical order and the natural merge – the *malkhut* ideal is realized. This is the main motif of *u-ve-khen ten pahdekha*, "Now put Your awe [upon all whom You have created]," and of the verses of kingship recited during *Musaf* on the Jewish New Year.

The Ten Commandments

The idea of God as leader, as political king intelligently accepted and submitted to, is seen in the revelation at Sinai. The Ten Commandments are unique because of their ethical character:

(1) The absence of the cult element is singular. Not one commandment refers to worship and ceremony. The ethos pervades the whole scene of Sinaitic revelation.

(2) Even the first five commandments, which refer to the God-man relationship, do not suggest to us any service or cult-performance, nor do they imply that God should be treated differently than the treatment accorded to man. There is a consistent parallelism between the first commandments and the last ones. The Rabbis noticed that the latter five commandments correspond to the first five.[2] Apparently God does not claim any privileges or unique rights. The same measure of honesty, loyalty, devotion which one owes to Him is due to one's fellow man as well, because covenant morality applies to both God and man. Therefore it is hardly possible to speak of ritual and cult in Judaism or of the traditional division of laws into *bein adam le-havero*, between man and his fellow man, and *bein adam la-makom*, between man and God. One and the same ethos regulates social interrelationships. Man's contact with God should be seen against the backdrop of human-divine society. Even His kingdom should be understood as a political reality located within society.

---

2. *Anokhi*, the first commandment, corresponds to *lo tirtzah* ("do not murder"), for the murderer reduces the divine image in the world; "do not steal" corresponds to "do not take the name of God in vain," for the thief will inevitably swear falsely in court, and so on. See *Song of Songs Rabbah* 4:5.

The double account of the covenant renewal at Sinai (Ex. 19–20 and 24) has led many radical Bible critics to the assertion that there were two reports about the Sinaitic revelation and that the Decalogue is a product of a later period; the original "Decalogue" must have dealt with cultic norms. But this distinction can be understood differently. There is no doubt that when Moses delivered his first message to Israel about the forthcoming revelation, the Jews, Egyptian slaves conversant with magical practices and ceremonials, understood their new relationship to God exclusively in terms of cult; they never expected a Decalogue as unique as that one embodying a strange ethos which was to substitute for the cultic relationship. The narrative of the event itself, both in Exodus and Deuteronomy, emphasizes the fear that overcame the people during the unfolding of the revelation-drama. Of course it is partially attributable to the numinous experience – "...therefore why should we die? for this great fire will consume us" (Deut. 5:22). Yet to some extent they were also horrified by the strange, incomprehensible content of the revealed message. Apparently, Moses found another covenant performance indispensable. He demanded a reacceptance of the covenant under a new aspect, the divine-human aspect.

> And Moses came and told the people all the words of the Lord, and all the judgments, and all the people answered with one voice, and said, "All the words which the Lord has said will we do." And Moses wrote all the words of the Lord, and rose up early in the morning, and built an altar under the hill, and twelve pillars, according to the twelve tribes of Israel.... And Moses took half of the blood, and put it in basins; and half of the blood he sprinkled on the altar. And he took the book of the covenant, and read in the hearing of the people: and they said, "All that the Lord has said we will do, and obey." And Moses took the blood, and sprinkled it on the people, and said, "Behold the blood of the covenant, which the Lord has made with you concerning all these words" (Ex. 24:3–8).

The new covenant renewal referred to the subject matter of the laws, to their character and content: to serve God through the realization of a unique ethos. The ceremony of sprinkling one part of the blood on the altar and the other one on the people symbolizes the merger of God and Israel, their association and communion. The divine royal-dominion is a comradeship kingdom, in which the king and the subjects enjoy identical prerogatives. It is a divine monarchy by the will of God and the people.

The attribute *E-lokei Yisrael* ("God of Israel") is mentioned in this narrative for the first time. The meaning of *Yisrael* is twofold:

(1) man emerged victorious from his encounter with deity – "...for you have contended with God and with men, and have prevailed" (Gen. 32:29).

(2) God rules.

Both meanings complete each other. *Yisrael* denotes the triumph of man over the numinous moment in his relationship with God, his victory over the antithetic phase in his communion with his Creator. Driven to utter absurdity and self-negation, entangled in a night-long conflict with a hostile transcendental being, at dawn he emerges a hero, winning the battle by reforming himself and changing the aspect. God becomes a comrade-king, a fellow-participant in the social drama, a member of a political society, whose unity was primarily forged by the realization of the covenant. *E-lokei Yisrael* conveys political rule; in such a social milieu man frees himself from the primordial horror instilled in him by the original sin, bridges the gap separating him from God, and establishes friendly communion with Him. Both are members of a theo-political society. There is closeness, intimacy and comradeship. God rules as a comrade-king. Man does not retreat before Him.

> And they saw *E-lokei Yisrael*... And upon the nobles of the children of Israel He laid not his hand; and they beheld God, and did eat and drink (Ex. 24:11).

The narrative emphasizes the reconciliation of man and God, the complete disappearance of the numinous, awe-inspiring moment. Man cannot see God and continue to exist. An approach that gets too close to God spells doom for man. The ancient curse of "I heard Your voice in the garden, and I was afraid, because I was naked; and I hid myself" (Gen. 3:10) emerged over the human being; at the realization of the covenant, it disappeared. God and man participate in one act of realization. The covenantal meal, the symbol of communion and coexisting, was consummated. They ate in the presence of God. They saw God and yet continued to exist. We also understand the symbolic act of building the altar of twelve stones. The diverse Jewish community was reunited under divine leadership as a theo-political society.

Conclusion

Now let us review the different phases through which the emergent human personality passes:

(1) Man as a biological being against his genetic background, animal in all its insistences and demands: the only difference between man and animal is the extent to which the technical intelligence has progressed. (Man as described in the first chapter of creation.)

(2) Man acquiring personality by experiencing the ethical norm and getting involved in sympathetic coexistence with the thou: man begins to separate from the natural realm and encounters in his subjective capacity an objective world. Ethical solidarity is characteristic of this stage. (Man as described in the second chapter of Genesis.)

(3) Man splitting his existence into an ethico-natural and orgiastic-demonic personality, introducing horror into the world and attempting to deceive his genuine ego (the original sin).

(4) The free, charismatic, anarchic and lonely personality, which revolts against man-made institutions and mores and discovers the moral law, chances later upon the God of morality and becomes acquainted with Him (Abraham).

(5) The historical personality which immortalizes itself through covenant historical reality by continuous self-revealing in the covenant society. At this stage man raises concrete naturalness to historicity.

(6) The antithetic charismatic personality of the interim period who is captivated and captured by the numinous God (Moses at the burning bush).

(7) The imprisoned charismatic personality freeing itself from numinous horror by retracing the footsteps of historical development or by identifying itself with the charismatic founder. The interim chosen personality reconstructs freedom out of historical necessity.

(8) The apostolic personality tied in by a bond of solidarity and sympathy with the God of the covenant. The apostolic personality is the redeemer who co-participates in the drama of realization. In other words, the man of the miracle appears: the harmonious personality that reconciles the natural with the historical order (Moses through the plagues and the exodus from Egypt).

(9) The theo-political personality, which asserts itself in a state-society that is dedicated to a single objective: to live in comradeship with God and to freely abide by His will. There is not only a covenant between God and man, but a socio-political bond as well. The religious ethos assumes a legal aspect; the subjective ethos becomes an objective moral law (Moses at the revelation at Sinai).

Index of Topics and Names

Index of Biblical and Rabbinic Sources